the booster
and
the snitch

the booster
and
the snitch

DEPARTMENT STORE SHOPLIFTING

MARY OWEN CAMERON

THE FREE PRESS OF GLENCOE

COLLIER-MACMILLAN LIMITED, *London*

To Kenneth and Kathleen

ACKNOWLEDGMENT

To the reader acquainted with sociological research, it will be obvious that some of the major concepts in this book have their source in the writings of the late Edwin H. Sutherland and his associates: Albert K. Cohen, Donald Cressey, Alfred Lindesmith, Henry McKay, Lloyd Ohlin, and Karl Schuessler. Prof. Schuessler directed the dissertation from which this book is an adaptation; I am especially grateful to him.

Mr. Loren Edwards made much of the research material that I used accessible. His cooperation made the study possible.

For help and moral support going well beyond his vows to love, honor, cherish, and give editorial advice, I am grateful to my husband, Kenneth Neill Cameron.

contents

CHARTS

MAPS

TABLES

EVERYONE likes to talk about shoplifting. Most people have been tempted to steal from stores, and many have been guilty (at least as children) of "snitching" an item or two from counter tops. With merchandise so attractively displayed in department stores and super markets, and much of it apparently there for the taking, one might ask why everyone isn't a thief. Fortunately for retail merchants, everyone isn't.

Almost everybody has a story or two about shoplifting. Most of them are apocryphal although they are told with great sincerity. Every town, if we are to believe these stories, has its little old kleptomaniac lady who steals at will and the merchandise is charged to her son's account (more about her later). Although folklore about shoplifting abounds, there has been no attempt to bring together the facts and to integrate them with our growing body of knowledge about crime in general.

The sequence of this study, which does attempt an integration, is in four stages:

(a) The anecdotal presentation of material on shoplifting drawn from reality;

(b) the facts (largely statistical) on shoplifting gathered chiefly from the private records of a large Chicago department store;

(c) a discussion of the relation of the operation of

private police to the data which comprise the public
records of larceny;

(d) the presentation of hypotheses attempting to explain
shoplifting and to relate the explanation of shoplifting to
explanations of other forms of crime.

As most merchants know, there are two major groups of
shoplifters: the commercial shoplifters, "boosters," and the
pilferers, "snitches." Boosters seem to differ little from other
professional thieves: they have well-defined contacts with
criminal subcultures, and they shift from one form of
illegal vocation to another. Conventional sociological explanations of other forms of crime seem to apply to "boost-
ing."

Pilferers, however, are quite different. If our data are
correct, they are chronic thieves who are "respectable"
citizens and have little or no contact with criminal groups.
They do not share the "values" and folkways of the professional thief. Neither are they the desperate poor stealing
from necessity. And, moreover, to confuse matters further,
they are *not* compulsive, neurotic personalities stealing out
of uncontrollable inner urges.

Because they fail to conform to any of our preconceived
notions of what criminals should be, pilferers are a very
interesting group. How are they to be explained. How do
explanations fits existing criminological theories? Or don't
they? To explain pilferers we may have to go beyond present
theories in the field of criminology.

**the booster
and
the snitch**

prologue

MRS. WELLS was a "booster"; but who was Sally Brown? The store police wondered and so did I as we waited for the (Chicago) city police van to come to take both of them to the women's "lockup." Sally just sat there weeping, clutching a hard wad of facial tissues.

The store detectives knew Mrs. Wells—intimately. They had arrested her before. Once when she had stolen a fur jacket; once again when she had attempted to carry out three women's suits (with hangers) fastened to a strap around her neck. In fact, when the store records had been checked, she had been apprehended by the detectives as a shoplifter fourteen times in ten years.

Mrs. Wells also knew the store protection staff. "Bill," she said, "your wife was having a baby when you picked me up the last time. How's everything?" Bill took out his wallet generously filled with baby pictures. Mrs. Wells looked at them with interest. "You know," she said to me, "I've got two boys of my own. One of them is a senior at

1

Purdue and the other graduated. He's an engineer in Korea
now."

She looked proud. "I've put both of my boys through
college."

"The hell you did," said Bill, "this store put them
through."

Mrs. Wells spoke with some heat. "I'd have been better
off if I'd stayed out of here. Everytime I get in this store,
you people jump me. I should have stuck to 'Monkey
Wards.'

"Listen," she continued, "when the van gets here, it's
going to be too late to call my attorney. I'm going to be in
the lockup all night. Can't you fix it so I won't have to be
put in the same room with her?" She pointed to Sally
Brown. "I know her kind. She's not going to let me sleep
ten minutes in the whole damn night. She'll cry and carry
on and try to make me think the whole world is coming to
an end."

"Can't do a thing for you," Bill said, but he handed Mrs.
Wells an extra packet of cigarettes. "This'll help you put
in the time anyway."

"Thanks," she said, "nothing personal, but you ought to
join an athletic club or something. You're getting that
middle-aged bulge."

Bill reddened a little.

The police van came up to the inconspicuous side exit
of the store where we were waiting. Mrs. Wells waved to
us and joined the woman detective who accompanied the
van. "Hello," she said, "you're new on this detail."

Sally Brown continued to clutch her wad of facial tissues.
She had not spoken nor, indeed, looked up, since we had
left the interrogation rooms on the tenth floor of the store.

Her face was swollen and blotched and she hiccuped from
sobbing. Passively she allowed herself to be led to the van.
The world outside her misery seemed lost to her.

Store detectives and police exchanged the necessary formal data to make the arrest official.

Mrs. Wells was charged with carrying away with larce-
nous intent one dozen grey cashmere sweaters. Sally Brown
was charged with the theft of a suitcase, nightgown, negli-
gee, cosmetic case, a pair of slippers, and three jars of face
cream.

But who was she?

To the store detectives, the name Brown, especially
Sally Brown, seemed like a "spur of the moment" name.
She carried no driver's license or other identification papers
(and her purse, person, and clothing had been thoroughly
searched by a woman detective). She had given her address
as the Hotel Maypole, and a phone call to the hotel indicated that a Miss Sally Brown had registered three days
before. She had brought no luggage with her, but had paid
her rent one week in advance. She had caused no disturbance.

Sally Brown was, perhaps, 35 years old; she was slender,
brunette, and smartly dressed. In her purse was about $300
in cash. There were no pawn tickets or locker keys. She
seemed by her behavior to know nothing of legal procedure.
I thought she was a pilferer (or, as Mrs. Wells would have
called her, "a snitch.") Her story was plausible, almost too
plausible, in fact, since none of it could be checked. She
told the store detectives that she had separated from her
husband ten days before and had come to Chicago to find
a job. After spending a week with a "boy friend" from Des
Moines (and she refused to say where she had stayed or

under what name) she had moved to the Maypole Hotel. She refused to give her husband's name or other information that would permit accurate identification. She admitted having stolen the merchandise but claimed that she had never before stolen anything and said that she was so "nervous" she didn't know what she was doing. "I intended to pay for it—really I did."

The store detectives checked prior arrest records in the store and in other stores in Chicago and found that no "Sally Brown" who exactly fitted her description had recently been arrested; the name was probably not her real name and it was so common that the "name check" was undoubtedly worthless. The only way to discover her identity was through the police who would take her fingerprints and thereby uncover any previous convictions for crimes.

Bill was fairly sure in his own mind that Sally Brown was a professional thief and that her distress was an act. I was inclined to believe her, but I was in the store as a sociologist trying to understand shoplifting. Hence I neither took sides nor offered an opinion.

Four other people had been arrested for shoplifting in the store that day. Three were adolescent girls arrested together, and when they were brought up to the interrogation rooms, they were a defiant group at first. Mrs. Kelly, one of the detectives, had observed them stealing costume jewelry and scarves. She followed them almost from the moment they entered the store. After they had helped themselves to ten or fifteen dollars worth of merchandise, Mrs. Kelly told the girls that they must come to the office. One tried to run away, but Mrs. Kelly had already summoned two other detectives who helped her with the arrest.

When the names, addresses, and phone numbers for the three were finally ascertained, their parents were called. The parents, professing great shock, agreed to come to the store to talk with the detectives. The store personnel also called the school guidance counselor who said that none of them had been in serious trouble before. The girls, by that time tearful and frightened, were released to their parents' custody. Thy were not "booked" with the juvenile court authorities.

Arnold R. was the other person arrested for shoplifting in the store that day. He had attempted to exchange his worn sport jacket for a new one. With forethought he had brought a razor blade to remove the tags conspicuously sewed to the sleeve and back of the new jacket. He erred in choosing a secluded corner of the store for this operation, a corner for this reason under constant observation by a detective.

When arrested and interrogated, Arnold produced adequate identification including his driver's license and social security card. Reluctantly he showed the stub of his pay check as a hospital orderly. A call to his landlady verified his address. He had lived there for two years. The "name check" in the cooperatively kept files of ten department stores established that he had not been arrested in any of them. A call to the personnel department of the hospital where he worked verified his claim to employment and even produced the information that he was a steady employee who would be a good risk for a charge account. (The detective who called, to save Arnold embarrassing explanations, implied he was from the credit department of the store.)

The store made no formal charge against Arnold, but he

left the store a chastened young man. Searched, examined
for evidence of narcotics addiction, looked at by many
members of the store protection staff, he knew that his
name had been recorded in the files of the store and in
the memories of the detectives. If ever he were to be apprehended for stealing again he would be sent to jail for a
long term. He was escorted to the door of the store and
warned that never, under any circumstances, was he to return to the store. The warning was not politely given.

The day was routine for the store protection staff. Aside
from shoplifters, they worked on the problem of merchandise missing from a place to which only employees were
given access. They also thought they had a lead on the
woman thief who specialized in stealing purses in the rest-
rooms. Her technique was ingenious. Dropping an earring
or lipstick under the door of a locked stall, she asked the
occupant's help in retrieving it. While the customer was
looking at the floor, she would reach over the top of the
stall and steal the occupant's purse from the hook on the
door. The thief's face had never been seen, but several
customers were certain they could identify her hand, arm,
and voice. Two women detectives were assigned to apprehend the thief. After a few very bitter comments on the
nature of their job, they accepted the assignment as part
of the next day's work.

Bill summed up the day; "One booster, one probable,
and four snitches. You thought we were too hard on the
Brown woman, didn't you?"

I admitted I thought Miss Brown was no more culpable
than Arnold R.

"Two'll get you ten she's got a record in Philadelphia,"
Bill said. "Didn't you see the label in her suit? She's prob-

ably a traveling professional. We don't get many of them in this store. You heard Wells say that boosters stay away from us. But when those Easterners hit Chicago, they think they're in the sticks and they'll clean out the place if we don't pick them up. Anyway she'll come up with a lawyer and we'll find out in a few days. Pro or not, she's a thief and it won't hurt her to cool off a little."

CHAPTER I

THE FIVE FINGER DISCOUNT

Theft and Inventory Shrinkage

EVERY DAY in Chicago (where this study was made), or in any other large city, hundreds and possibly even thousands of people who have not so far been the subject of adequate criminological study commit larceny from retail merchants. Some are employees; some are shoplifters; some are professional thieves who specialize in taking merchandise from stockrooms and warehouses. The aggregate "take" of their theft is enormous. Twelve department stores in New York City, for example, collectively estimated as theft losses for the year 1951 about $10,000,000.[1] A store executive said in an interview, "If we actually knew what is being stolen we would probably lose our minds."

Loren Edwards, the former head of the store protection division of a large Chicago department store writes as follows:

"We lose more money by stock shortage than we make. . . ." This statement, meaning that shrinkage was greater than

1. New York *Herald Tribune*, October 30, 1952.

profit, was made by a store comptroller at a comptroller's meeting.

Another store comptroller made the statement that "shoplifting in stores comprises 30% of all inventory shrinkage or loss." The theory has also been advanced that the major part of losses, due to theft, is caused by dishonest employees.

One expert in the field of shrinkage prevention has estimated that a fantastic sum of money—$1,700,000,000—is stolen from retailers each year. Another estimate was that approximately 100,000 thefts, at an average take of $15.00 each, are committed nationally each week. That figure would add up to $78,000,000 a year. In my opinion this is a very conservative figure.[2]

The reason for the great divergence in the "estimates" is to be found in department store and specialty store accounting practices: losses due to theft become part of a general, undifferentiated figure composed of several factors and known as "inventory shrinkage" or "inventory shortage." Inventory shrinkage is calculated by taking the difference between the retail price for merchandise, as assigned by store management, and the actual amount realized on the sale of the merchandise. It is usually reported as a per cent of gross sales volume. Thus a store with total receipts of $10,000,000 a year and an inventory shrinkage of $20,000 will calculate its loss as two per cent. In urban department store merchandising, a 2 per cent loss is generally considered a "good" figure. Some large department stores admit to shrinkage figures of 5 per cent or higher.

Inventory shrinkage is not wholly a result of theft. It may include losses due to price markdowns which occur when, for example, an item becomes shopworn or "dated" and is, at the discretion of a department manager, sold for

2. Edwards, Loren. *Shoplifting and Shrinkage Protection for Stores.* (Springfield, Ill., 1958), p. v.

less than the assigned price. Losses resulting from the disappearance of money or merchandise are also a part of inventory shrinkage. The word "disappearence" is used advisedly. It could possibly mean that the merchandise was "purchased" by a buyer but never really delivered to the store. A "paper deal" could have been contracted by a "responsible" employee.

In many departments of a large department store, price markdown clearly accounts for a smaller proportion of inventory shrinkage than theft; in other departments price markdown is presumed by the management to be a major component of inventory shrinkage.

Inventory shrinkage, then, is the index regularly used by merchants as a general measure for many forms of loss. Unfortunately, it is seldom a specific measure of theft and never a measure capable of differentiating between the different kinds of theft. Therefore it is impossible for store management, or anyone else, to specify accurately the amount of loss resulting from any particular component. Even if one is able to make some rough estimate of how much loss is due to theft and how much to markdown, it is impossible to give more than a semi-informed guess as to how much theft is the result of shoplifters and how much theft is the result of employees.

Employee theft, it is generally agreed, is a large component, probably greater, perhaps much greater than shoplifting itself. Currently, store protection personnel speak of the "generally accepted" figure of 75 per cent of all theft as employee theft. Although this percentage may be "generally accepted," it is not, certainly, accurate. Some kinds of merchandise can be easily stolen by sales employees; some is more easily stolen from stockrooms and storage; still other merchandise is especially accessible to knowledgeable shoplifters. While a store with many departments may average out losses and arrive at a "generally accepted" figure, a specialty store's losses could run from zero to 100 per cent as a result of any possible component. Only a careful analysis of each department's or each store's particular problems can be useful in cutting the losses in that store or that department.

Store employees certainly have many opportunities to steal money, to carry out merchandise, or to pass merchandise on to confederates. The arrest of an employee for theft and a search of his lodgings often reveals large amounts of stolen merchandise, sometimes amounting to several thousands of dollars in value. The stolen merchandise recovered from the apartment of a teen-age boy who had worked in the camera section of a department store for six months included twenty suits, racks of neckties, forty-two cameras, and closets full of sheets, blankets, towels, shoes, underwear, cooking utensils, women's wear, etc. He had devised a not very foolproof but temporarily workable system of forging sales receipts with which his girl friend then obtained merchandise. Loren Edwards writes of this problem:

Fidelity and surety companies have issued statements, at different times, estimating that employee dishonesty costs American business over a half billion dollars a year. These estimates usually cover fidelity losses that have been reported. It would be impossible to estimate the unknown amount of pilferage of merchandise from stores, by employees.[3]

Donald Laird reports in *The Management Review:*[4]

3. *Ibid.*, p. 61.
4. "Psychology and the Crooked Employee," *The Management Review*. April, 1950.

One eastern drug chain had a $1,400,000 inventory loss in six months so the management used lie detectors on its 1,400 employees. It was found that nearly three-fourths of the employees had been helping themselves to merchandise and petty cash. Such surveys seem to indicate that small-scale theft, cheating, lying is prevalent in about 60% of the population.

Warehouse and stockroom theft may involve either employees or outsiders, and the operation of these thieves can cause large amounts of merchandise to disappear in a short period of time. There does not appear, however, to be any generally accepted estimate of the amount of loss resulting from this type of theft. One of the estimates is that of Norman Jaspan, President of Norman Jaspan Associates, who is quoted in the April 24, 1961 issue of *The Electrical Merchandising Week* as saying: "Over the years the cost of . . . malpractices by employees has been getting progressively greater until it has reached a total of $1,000,000,000 a year just in cash and goods." Jaspan's investigations, which he states were made over a period of 37 years, led him to believe that seventy per cent of inventory shortages were the result of employee malpractices; twenty-five percent he believed were the result of honest clerical errors and the remainder a result of shoplifting. Jaspan's estimates for different merchandising units were as follows:

Type of Store	Total $ value of sales	Loss resulting from employee dishonesty
Department stores	16,000,000,000	140,000,000
Supermarkets	50,000,000,000	100,000,000
Hardware stores	9,000,000,000	90,000,000
Discount houses	4,500,000,000	25,000,000
Variety stores	4,000,000,000	60,000,000
Drug retailers	6,000,000,000	50,000,000
Others	135,000,000,000	140,000,000

Jaspan attributed the majority of these losses to employees at supervisory levels.

E. B. Weiss writing in the December, 1958 issue of *Advertising Age* also argued that shoplifting is a minor factor: "If shopper pilferage were totally eliminated it would hardly make a dent in the total shortage factor! . . . Store employees of all ranks out-steal the shopper."

He called for a "deep study of shopper pilferage."

Perhaps some day the great manufacturing associations in food, drug, soft and hard goods will come together and underwrite a study to be made by a competent firm of auditors-investigators. I am positive that statistics will leave not the slightest doubt that the real culprit in stock shortages is not the shopper—but the retailer, his policies and practices, and his staff.

He believed that many retail merchants indulge in the luxury of poor control, poor personnel practices, and poor accounting practices. Mr. Weiss noted that one department store with an annual turnover of about $17,000,000 reported stock shortage of 1.3 per cent. When a more competent audit was made, losses were, in fact, 2.9 percent. In housewares losses were 9 per cent and in cosmetics 5 per cent.

Impressions gathered in the course of the present study also support the view that employee theft far outranks shoplifting as a source of loss to retail merchants. Be this as it may, shoplifting is still a considerable source of loss, and more important from the point of view of this study, a major form of crime. How *major* has been obscured by the fact that it is handled by private rather than public police. As a result, arrests for shoplifting (or of employees for stealing) seldom come to the public attention and seldom become part of the public records which form the basis for most crime statistics.

Detectives employed by a single downtown department store in Chicago, for example, arrested two thirds as many adult women for shoplifting in that store in 1944 and again in 1945 as those shown in the official statistics on larceny as being formally charged by the police with petty larceny of all forms (including shoplifting) in the entire city of Chicago. [See p. 123]. This figure becomes even more impressive if one assumes store detectives are correct in believing that perhaps they apprehend only about one person out of every ten who shoplift on any particular day.

HANDLING THE SHOPLIFTING PROBLEM

Since so little has been written in the serious literature of criminology about shoplifting, and since such erroneous impressions are gained from folklore and popular literature on the subject, some description of this form of larceny as it exists in actual practice must be presented at the outset. Information for this presentation has been acquired mainly in conversation with retail merchants and managers of retail chain stores.

Throughout any urban area, retail store owners or managers realize from time to time that certain items of merchandise are unaccountably missing. When a storekeeper, for instance, believes that losses are especially heavy, he may keep track of particular objects and discover to his dismay that of a dozen toothbrushes or cigarette lighters that were placed on display, six remain, two were sold, and four are gone and unaccounted for. All kinds of merchandise, from toys to television sets disappear. Occasionally the merchant sees someone steal an item. His reaction then depends on himself and the thief. There is no standardized way of meeting the situation, but the one thing the merchant seldom does is to call the police.

Independent merchants empirically develop their own methods of dealing with shoplifters. One grocer said that when he sees an adult lifting something, he adds $5.00 to the grocery bill. When the thief asks, "What is this?" the grocer answers significantly, "You know." And he suggests that perhaps the "customer" would rather leave and do his shopping elsewhere. A druggist reported that he always asks to wrap *the rest* of the "customer's" merchandise, pointedly emphasizing the words. If the thief fails to produce the stolen merchandise, the druggist says emphatically, "I'll keep *you* in mind." A hardware retailer reported that he uses the direct approach, "Look, I got eyes. You took two paring knives. Pay me for them."

The manager of a large bookstore in New York reported that while the store personnel never arrest a shoplifter, sales clerks are instructed to "breathe down the neck" of anyone suspected of stealing. A suspected thief is watched so carefully—even obviously—that he goes away.

Most independent merchants seem to believe that after having once tactfully let a thief know that he has been "spotted," he will never return to the store.

Larger merchandising enterprises, chain grocery, drug, variety stores, appliance shops and the like usually follow the same system of dealing with shoplifters as do small independent retailers. When a clerk sees merchandise being stolen, he is usually instructed to notify the manager who personally "suggests" to the thief that the merchandise be paid for or returned. In a chain store in which inventory shrinkage exceeds an allotted limit, private detectives may be called in to arrest some of the offenders and occasionally formal charges of arrest are placed against shoplifters.

In some branches of retail merchandising, on the other hand, store protection officials admit ruefully that inventory shortage is no problem. One large chain of bookdealers reported less than .5 per cent loss. Instead of regarding this minuscule loss as a cause for rejoicing, it was regarded as the result of "old fashioned" merchandising methods including much personal service by a large staff of sales clerks. "Certainly," said the security representative, "we have a small inventory shortage, but our payroll for sales personnel cuts our profit to almost nothing. We could be ahead by accepting the inevitability of shoplifting. Self-service plus all the losses it will bring will net us more profit in the long run than individualized service with almost no loss at all."

As compared with retail booksellers, it is worth noting, public libraries (with books on supermarket-type open shelves in the privacy of stacks and with almost no security precautions) have only minor pilferage problems. One large urban library system reported that its losses in all forms of pilferage (failure of borrowers to return books, theft from open stacks, etc.) represented less than one per cent of its holdings for circulation (and less than .05 per cent of its actual circulation).

But the trend toward self-service supermarkets in the retail grocery business as well as in other retail merchandising in the last two decades has made "foodlifting" a fairly profitable field attracting even "professional" shoplifters. Food store detectives tell of thieves carrying out a dozen steaks at a time or large quantities of canned fish, turkey, or other "fancy" goods.[5]

Retail trade journals indicate an increasing concern with shoplifting in stores that deal in specialized items: phonographs, tape recorders, records, electric shavers, cameras, and camera supplies. In many of these stores modern merchandising methods relying on self-service have cut the sales staff, but in some types of retail sales a substantial part of the resulting saving has been absorbed by inventory shrinkage. As self-service rises, store personnel increasingly find themselves at a loss for methods of dealing with theft.

Just as in the past when safe manufacturers and safe crackers ran a see-saw race for what resulted in a now virtually crack-proof safe, manufacturers and thieves have turned to a duel over the packaging of goods. A symposium in the August, 1959 issue of *Modern Packaging*, recommends measures to reduce pilferage. Multiple packaging, i.e., putting six bars of soap into a single bag reduces the likelihood of pilferage. One bar of soap is easily slipped into a pocket —not so, six. Wrapping fresh fruit will prevent the housewife from selecting the top layer of strawberries from each pint box and making up a box of her own with nothing but top grade berries (the exact nature of the dishonesty involved here may escape most housewives and readers). Gluing small packages such as razor blades on outsized cards will prevent their pilferage. In fact, a survey by Pax Fax Inc. (reported in the article above) found that, regardless of value, merchandise in small packages was more often pilfered than the same merchandise wrapped in or glued to large packages.

5. For an interesting descriptive article "foodlifting" see, Bill Fay (of the Jewel Food Company in Chicago), "I Am a Supermarket Detective," *Collier's*. March 29, 1952.

Other supermarket "tricks" of pilferers include filling the deceptively large boxes of soap flakes or cereal to the brim from other boxes, and switching caps (on which prices are stamped) of small bottles of hand lotion or shampoo to large bottles having the same size cap. Dave Chapman, a leading packager says, "The philosophy of self-service and open-rack merchandising is predicated on the increase in sales appeal by removing the inhibitants between the consumer and the product. The closer we get the consumer to the product, the higher the chance he will buy."[6] The higher the chance, too, that he will steal.

The trade journals of camera and phonographic supply organizations report that shoplifters are "taking everything that isn't nailed down." Transistor radios, tape recorders, and small TV sets as well as cameras, film, audio tape, and records can "be kissed goodbye" if they are unattended for a moment. The trend toward miniaturization of equipment for audio and visual recording is of great help to the thief. Characteristically these equipment shops turn to more equipment as an answer to theft—protection equipment. Trade journals advertise closed-circuit TV installations to discourage pilfering and frequently store managers work out ways to hook all display models of small radios, TVs, and the like to a single circuit which, when broken by the removal of any one set, sounds an alarm. One such a protection device sells for $15.00 and is the size of a cigar box. Mounted on an electrical wall outlet, demonstrator sets are plugged into it. If the plug of a radio is pulled out, a light or a buzzer is set off.

Convex, regular, and "one way" mirrors are used by many retail merchants to keep their stock under observa-

6. *Modern Packaging.* August, 1959.

tion from a distance or from around corners. For remote alcoves in specialty shops invisible infrared circuits can be set up to warn sales personnel that someone has entered the alcove. Customers are also often asked to check their brief cases and shopping bags. For the legitimate customer, this can sometimes be made to seem a service; the potential shoplifter who refuses to check his luggage is thus more easily recognized.

Even in the most modern retail bookstores valuable art books are still kept behind counters, as much, however, to protect the books from vandalism as from theft. Books on sex and marriage "simply walk off" unless they are kept in locked cases. "Perhaps," a store manager hazarded, "people are embarrassed to buy these books. Theft may seem a less difficult means of acquiring them."

But once a shoplifter is detected, all stores face the same problem of knowing how to deal with him. Children who pilfer are often treated more severely and directly than adults. They are usually scolded, their names recorded, and their parents notified. They may be warned not to come into the store again and threatened with police action if they do.

The caution with which adult shoplifters must be treated and the more severe treatment accorded children reflect a general problem that confronts the shoplifting victim. Whether he is a small owner-merchant, the store manager of a nationwide retail chain, or a store detective, in dealing with adults the victim must understand the law of arrest if he is, in fact, going to stop or arrest a thief.

Technically and legally any citizen who sees a crime being committed, whether felony or misdemeanor, has the right and indeed, the obligation to halt (arrest) the criminal or to assist in his arrest. In exercising this right, however, the citizen must be certain that he observes the proper legal forms. He may otherwise be committing an act of false arrest.

In the common law, the power of arrest resided almost equally in the police and the ordinary citizen. The legal right of arrest was as follows: Arrests could be made on warrants, or written orders of the court, by anyone authorized to serve them. Arrests could be made without such warrants on two conditions: (a) that a crime was known to have been committed and (b) that the crime was committed in the presence of the person making the arrest, or, in case the crime was a felony and was not committed in the presence of the arresting officer, he had good reason to suspect that the person arrested was guilty. That is, a person committing a misdemeanor could not be arrested, except on warrant, by anyone, police officer or other, not present when the offense was being committed; a person suspected of having committed a felony might be arrested by one who was not present when the felony was committed, provided he had positive knowledge that a felony had been committed by someone and had good reason to suspect that this was the guilty person. This is the general law of arrest, which has been modified somewhat by statutes.[7]

False arrest, slander, forcible detention, and even kidnaping charges can be instituted against a person who makes a citizen arrest. This is not a problem equally faced by the public police who are relatively immune to civil suits for damages. In a citizen arrest, when direct accusation is made, the store owner, manager, or owner's representative may become involved in an expensive and time-consuming law suit. Should the owner or his employee have made an error, albeit an honest error, or for any reason be unable

7. Sutherland, Edwin H. *Principles of Criminology.* (Philadelphia, 1939), pp. 233–234.

to prove the charge, there might be heavy damages to pay to the arrested person. A defense attorney may make the charge quite difficult to prove since the arresting citizen seldom knows adequately the laws of evidence. For two paring knives or a package of candy, or even for more expensive items, the merchant often reasons, the risk is not worth taking.*

In Illinois, prior to the shoplifting law effective in 1957 (subsequent to the time the arrests studied here were made), a merchant or his representative faced the danger of a law suit for false arrest if he detained an innocent person. This remains the common practice in most States. Edwards writes:

In case of arrest or detention it was necessary to prove to a court or a jury that a crime actually had been committed in the presence of the arrester, and that the arrested person was guilty. Failure to do this, and if prosecution should fail, the merchant could be liable for false arrest or false imprisonment, and be required to pay civil damages. For this reason, some merchants, including nationally known retail organizations, took no action against shoplifters.

The laws of many of the states similarly restrict merchants in the protection of their property; however some states recognize a middle ground which can be used as a partial solution to the shoplifting problem, while at the same time preserving the rights of a person arrested.

This middle ground allows a merchant to detain a person if

---

* Although clarity for the reader might call for the use of separate words to indicate "store arrest" or "citizen arrest" vs official police arrest, the word "arrest" has been chosen deliberately for both kinds of arrest, and distinctions will be made by the adjective when these distinctions are necessary and not already clear from the context. In either case a thief is "arrested" or stopped in the act of larceny and the arresting citizen or officer must have seen the offender commit the offense. Citizen or police officer, he must be prepared to testify to this in court.

he has probable cause, not mere suspicion, for believing that the person detained has unlawfully appropriated merchandise. The detention must be limited to a reasonable time.[8]

Most States are more strict. An Ohio appellate court even had to rule that the actions of a store manager did not amount to false arrest when he approached a customer and said, "Madam, that bag will have to be searched." The court ruled that the defendant company

thought its private right to property was being violated, which it was resisting. It was not assuming to vindicate any public right. The plaintiff was not accused of any crime. Nothing was done to indicate that she was being held for delivery to a peace officer to answer criminal charge. Under such circumstances there is no basis for the suggestion that this is a false imprisonment, indicated by false arrest. [Lester v Albers Super Markets. *Ohio Appeals* 114 N.E. (2) 529, 1952, p. 532.]

Only rarely in relation to the total number of arrests for shoplifting by private police do public police make arrests other than "technical" bookings made on the complaint of store personnel. The main functions of the "store detail" of an urban detective force are to trace professional shoplifting troupes and their "fences"; and to convey persons already arrested by private police to a place of confinement prior to their establishing bail.

Of the many adults and children who commit larceny by shoplifting on any particular day, only a few are actually seen. Of those who are seen, many are handled by implied threat. Only a few shoplifters, seen by store managers actually taking especially valuable merchandise or those who are seen by private detectives, are ever arrested. Of the number arrested by citizen arrest (and this includes arrests

8. Edwards, *op. cit.*, p. 176.

made by private detectives), only an unknown proportion (store officials estimate between 10 per cent and 35 per cent) are prosecuted and thus have their records incorporated into official criminal statistics. Shoplifters who are not caught, of course, and those who are "caught" but not arrested by store managements, form an unknown and actually unknowable segment of the criminal—or quasicriminal—population.

PEOPLE WHO BECOME "DATA"

The present study presents an analysis (largely from statistical evidence) of two main samples of the "knowable" class of shoplifters. The first segment of data consists of a sample (called the "Store" sample) of one out of four of the shoplifters arrested by detectives of one department store in the eight year period 1943–1950. The department store from which this sample of arrests is used will be referred to as the Store (capital "S") or Lakeside Co. Department stores are naturally reluctant to have this punitive phase of their activity become the subject of public discussion, but the validity of the results is in no way affected by the anonymity of the Store. Disguising the name, as is done in this case, is no different in principle from the usual practice of eliminating or disguising names in case history reports.)

The second major sample of shoplifting arrests used in this study (called the "Womens' court" sample) is composed of the adult women who were seen, arrested, and *formally charged* with "petty larceny, shoplifting" by all the stores in the city of Chicago for the three year period

1948–1950. Some data on men arrested for shoplifting and prosecuted in the Municipal Court were also obtained, and some information taken from police arrest records of shoplifters is given.

Although these data, coming as they do from specific (and available) sources, cannot be taken as representative of the total group of shoplifters, they nevertheless form the most adequate data so far available on shoplifting.

Since one of the major objectives of this study will be the analysis of factors which bias the statistical records of both "Store" and "court" samples (an objective which can best be realized as the records are themselves presented), there will be little attempt to discuss biasing factors prior to the presentation of the data. It seems useful, however, to make an exception in regard to the "place bias" already touched upon (those shoplifters who happen to steal at stores employing detectives are almost the only ones arrested) and to emphasize the range and variety of selective factors that bring about the arrest of a shoplifter and perhaps bring him to official attention.

Aside from stealing at a store in which arrests are made by managers, proprietors, or private police, in order to be apprehended, the shoplifter must also come under the direct observation of the arresting person. Even when closed-circuit television is used, the person who steals one object and is observed on the television screen must usually be followed by a detective until he steals another article while under the direct observation of the detective. (Although, as noted above, the laws of arrest differ markedly in different States.) The risk to store management of being deliberately "framed" into a "false" arrest by the thief is always present. The risk to the store varies in accordance with the social status of the offender. The apparent marks of social status (dress, grooming, age, race, etc.) influence the detectives or store managers who must file the formal charge of arrest.

Detectives must see the act of shoplifting take place in order to make an arrest, and detectives cannot be equally observant of all persons in the store. (In some department stores, Lakeside Co. among them, sales clerks are rewarded by the management for "tips" to detectives on thieves, but the proportion of shoplifters arrested as a result of such tips is low—12 per cent for Lakeside Co. Actually, the chief objective of the tip procedure is not to detect shoplifters but to use employees to detect fellow employees who commit violations of trust, including stealing merchandise.)

Shoplifters arrested by store detectives, then, are usually persons who are deliberately watched or those the detectives "just happen" to see. Since the detectives' methods of operation determine who will be arrested, the question of the types of person they are "likely to see" is of considerable importance.

In department stores the detectives are mainly women. On duty they wear hats and coats, carry handbags and try to look like typical shoppers. Detectives are distributed one or two to a floor or section in the large stores (except for sections that are devoted to furniture, carpets, yard goods, and other relatively "non-shopliftable" merchandise).

Detectives frequently have duties to perform that involve the safety of staff and customers as well as the protection of merchandise; they are not engaged solely for the detection of shoplifters. If a lighted match is carelessly or deliberately thrown into a trash bin and a fire results, the store protection person is summoned by the sales clerk. If an elevator fails to function or an escalator becomes jammed, the first person on the scene will usually be "store protection." If a heart attack, fainting spell, or epileptic seizure occurs, among customers or employees, the call goes to store protection immediately. Or when customers quarrel and fight over a bargain, "I saw it first," store protection enters the scene to calm upset tempers. The efficient store detective, too, knows that any one of these emergencies may have been created for the purpose of taking him away from what could soon be the scene of a crime. An immediate call for help goes to the central office to bring other store detectives to the spot.

The chief "first floor" operator in a large urban store stated that in one month she and her assistants encountered alcoholics and narcotics addicts dashing in to steal merchandise. They also helped a person who had wandered into the store and collapsed as a result of a concussion following an automobile accident outside the store. A man was seen indecently exposing himself. And a fatal heart attack occurred. Along with these events, shoplifting, purse-snatching, and pocket-picking continued.

Store detectives are somewhat free to move about and to station themselves wherever experience has shown they will be most successful in their multitudinous assignments. On a floor where costume jewelry is displayed, for example, a detective frequently stands at the counter. While apparently just another customer also trying on jewelry, she is actually watching for someone to "pocket" or to put on and wear something away. She will be particularly attentive when merchandise falls or is pushed onto the floor,

for this is done intentionally by thieves so that they can be
concealed from the clerks while hiding merchandise in a
shopping bag or a handbag. When a shoplifter is seen
concealing merchandise or leaving the counter with it, he
(or she) will be followed from the department and perhaps from the store before being arrested. For relatively
inexpensive items, the thief will probably not be arrested
then but will be followed. If a single object of small value
is the only theft, the thief may even be allowed to leave
the store without being arrested. The danger of error in
arrest, and the hazards of deliberate enticement into making false arrests, are comparatively too great to risk arresting a person who has stolen only an inexpensive piece of
merchandise.

A man, for example, was observed by the writer and a
store detective pocketing a snakeskin billfold valued at
$24.00. The store detective, who observed the man acting
very suspiciously and conspicuously, did not arrest him.
She had observed that he wore a "trench coat" which undoubtedly had doublepocket openings leading to his suit
pockets or to the floor. She assumed, correctly it appeared
later, that the thief's motivation was to be arrested after
having "thrown" the merchandise (kicked the billfold into
an inconspicuous corner). Perhaps he would have resisted
arrest and forced the detective to injure him (such cases
have occurred before) in the arrest proceedings. He might
even have stationed seemingly reputable witnesses in stra-
tegic locations to observe the damage inflicted upon him.
He could therefore become the plaintiff in a suit for large
damages from the store. In this particular case, at least,
the store detective pointed out that the thief had indeed
"thrown" the stolen billfold by the simple expedient of

placing it between his sets of pockets and allowing it to fall to the floor. If captured, there would be no evidence of stolen merchandise on his person: he would have seemed to be an innocent victim of an overenthusiastic store detective and the store would have been the victim of a cleverly arranged suit for false arrest.

An experienced store detective made the interesting observation that most thieves once they are outside of the store and believe themselves beyond the range of observation of store detectives remove the stolen merchandise from parcels or pockets and examine it. When this examination takes place on a street corner or on a public conveyance, as it frequently docs, the detective who has followed the thief then makes his arrest. If the thief proceeds to the privacy of his own home without showing incriminating evidence, he has less likelihood of being caught.

In sections of a department store where the technique is applicable, and especially for the "gift" departments during the Christmas season, one-way mirrors and peep holes (through which, in either case, the operator can see without being seen) may make up a part of the ornamentation. The usefulness of this technique, however, is limited, as is closed-circuit television. In order to arrest a shoplifter who has been seen stealing merchandise, the operator behind the mirror must either have some way of signaling to another on the floor, or the operator must let the shoplifter out of his sight for the period of time it takes him to get from his hiding place to the shoplifter. This is undesirable since the thief may, during this time, have changed his mind, or passed the merchandise to a confederate or may deliberately have "thrown" the merchandise to invite false arrest.

In departments where especially valuable items are displayed: fur coats, silver, cameras, luggage, etc., operators may be especially stationed to guard these things. There they often function best by looking, to the initiated, conspicuously like plain clothes detectives or they may even wear uniforms. One detective to whom I was introduced—she looked like an unflattering stereotype of a prison matron or a female "cop"—said that she had been "in furs" for six years. "No," she said, "I've never arrested anyone. I just come here every day and either sit where people can see me or just walk around and look at people suspiciously. The insurance company requires a guard, and I'm it."

Many stores station uniformed police at exits. Again their service is prevention and assistance in arrest rather than detection.

Aside from watching merchandise being handled by customers, operators follow and observe "likely" suspects. They develop, they believe, after years of experience on their job, a "sixth sense" for people who are intending to steal. Certain mannerisms of the shoplifter are sometimes clues. The typical shopper looks at merchandise and ignores other people in the store; the shoplifter constantly watches people in order to know whether or not he is being observed or followed. When the store detective observes a "customer" looking at people rather than merchandise, he may follow the person, unobtrusively of course, through the store. Among other specific clues that the store detectives look for are shopping bags, knitting bags, brief cases, large purses, etc., within which merchandise may be concealed. Large bags with the store label (hat bags and the like) that appear to be crinkled or to have been folded and refolded may have been acquired by shoplifters and kept

for shoplifting tours. Persons with such "luggage" are carefully observed. Detectives also look for signs of tension and
strain.

Another group of people considered "likely" suspects
and watched by most department store detectives are unaccompanied adolescents. In many stores adolescent groups
are under almost constant observation, and this practice,
according to detectives, proves worth while. It is also a
distorting factor in statistical generalizations that involve
frequency of arrest.

Negro people are also kept under much closer observation
than whites. It is clear that here, too, the selective observations of store detectives constitute a source for distortion of
arrest statistics. One cannot measure this bias nor the bias
against adolescents and evaluate its importance by any objective standard, but it is unquestionably present and is a
factor of some significance in influencing the selection of
persons to be arrested. Racial bias is general and not especially characteristic of any particular store. Operators who
have worked in several stores and in different cities have the
same outlook and the same prejudices. Shoplifters who
blend into the dominant group of shoppers are less likely
to be noticed. The woman shoplifter who appears to be
well-to-do and carries herself with poise and assurance is
least likely to be observed, or apprehended even if she is
observed. A detective must be very sure of his evidence
before he risks the arrest of someone he believes to have no
prior criminal record, or possibly may have connections in
high places, and be able to obtain first-rate legal counsel.

To summarize: the distorting factors in arrest statistics
that have been touched on so far have included five points:
Some stores employ detectives empowered to make arrests

and others do not; the stationing and operating methods
of detectives employed by stores influence what they see
being stolen; the anti-Negro attitude of many detectives increases the chance of their seeing Negro shoplifters; adolescents are more frequently under observation than adults;
and finally, the caution the store detective feels he must
exercise in arresting anyone is enhanced when the suspected
thief appears to be "respectable."

These distorting factors probably apply generally to all
stores as well as department stores. They operate to select
out of the general run of shoplifters those who will have
any action taken against them. They are, in a sense, accidental or unconscious selective factors. But in the step
which occurs between store arrest, once made, and court
procedure, selective screening is deliberately and consciously introduced.

When inventory shrinkage is particularly high, store officials announce, sometimes stridently, that all apprehended shoplifters will be prosecuted. They may even post
signs to this effect. They believe that "word gets around"
and that shoplifters will go elsewhere. These assertions are
not, however, to be taken at face value.

Store police cannot formally charge all persons who
are arrested. Since testimony in court takes up the time of
store detectives, department store staff generally wish to
prosecute as few arrested persons as possible. The problem
is much the same for stores everywhere.

It will surprise people to learn that one important London
store lost between £15,000 and £20,000 last year through petty
pilfering. . . . Arrests are made but few thieves are charged, for
when a summons is issued the head of the department involved

and at least one of his assistants, must attend the court, which means the staff is shorthanded for several days. An average of twenty thieves are caught weekly in a large department store, and were all charged the directors would be faced with a total of at least 1,040 court cases a year. Suppose it were decided to proceed in all these cases and suppose an average of two witnesses were needed on each charge, and suppose in each case only two days were needed on each charge, and suppose in each case only two witnesses were needed, the firm would still lose 4,160 working days in the year. It is obvious that under these circumstances no firm can afford to push a campaign against the shoplifter.[9]

In the Chicago Municipal Court, a misdemeanant court, procedures are somewhat less time consuming than in the British court described by Cecil Bishop. But if the defendant demands, as he may, a jury trial, or if he obtains continuances of his case, several man-days of detectives' time may be wasted, from the store viewpoint, in court. Even a routine case requires at least half a day of detectives' time.

All large stores, then, face the problem of who among those who have been caught is to be prosecuted. The actual method of selection, however, is, in some degree, arbitrary and "intuitional." The store protection official who is judge of this process acts on an individual basis and without following any necessary rules of precedence. A social worker at the Chicago Municipal Court said that after twenty years' experience of seeing shoplifters being tried, she had yet to discover any principles underlying what appeared to be "sheer caprice" on the part of department store staffs. "Sometimes," she said, "one store will have its detectives in court testifying every day of the week. And

9. Bishop, Cecil. *Women and Crime*. (London, 1931), p. 6–7.

another time only a few well-known professionals will be brought in."

Although "sheer caprice" may have some hand in the selective screening procedure, some general principles operate also. Individuals are screened within a context which makes it desirable to prosecute as few persons as possible and still to protect merchandise from theft and the store from suits for false arrest. In determining whether or not a person is to be formally charged or released without charge, store officials look at two different problems: they wish to prosecute thieves who are shoplifting commercially, and they need to obtain a conviction in court.

If the arrested shoplifter is likely to be a person stealing merchandise in order to sell it or to return it for refund of the "purchase" price, he is almost certain to be formally charged. The evidence pointing toward "commercial" theft that interrogators look for includes a catalogue of items such as inadequate or inaccurate personal identification. A thief may carry a driver's license or other identifying documents belonging to someone whose pocket he has picked earlier in the day. Failure of the thief to live up to all aspects of his "identification" is cause for further interrogation at the very least. The thief who gives an out-of-town address or a hotel address may well be a *professional* thief. Pawn tickets, keys to public lockers, and the like are sure to be followed through by a thorough search of the places indicated before the shoplifter is allowed to walk out of the store. The nature and value of the stolen merchandise and special equipment for stealing or concealing merchandise is considered in determining whether the detective is confronted with commercial theft. Store detectives also observe the thief's behavior during the time he is being followed. They know that an experienced thief, having stolen merchandise of value will often go *up* an escalator rather than immediately *down* and out of the store. The thief will discover in this way whether or not he is being followed. He will also try to find a place where he can conceal himself and remove price tags or other incriminating labels. Staircases, rest rooms, and telephone booths are usually the most available places; hence they are watched with some care. Store detectives also look for narcotics addiction as evidence by behavior, by needle marks, or by the possession of narcotics.

While it is clearly in the interest of department stores to prosecute commercial shoplifters, they must also have a voluntary statement or a court finding of guilt for every arrested person. Those who refuse to sign a confession and a waiver of suit against the store must be prosecuted in the court. Only when a shoplifter has signed a confession of guilt—or has been found guilty by the court—is the store free from suit for false arrest. Although a shoplifter may be an obvious novice, he must still be prosecuted if he refuses to absolve the store from guilt in apprehending him.

Aside from protective and financial considerations, other factors sometimes influence the decision to prosecute or release. Occasionally, for instance, prosecution is used as a means of getting a severely disturbed neurotic or psychotic person to a source of adequate medical care. The court can, and sometimes does, refer arrested persons to the psychiatric division.

The overall number of formal charges made by a particular store may be subject to considerable variation. The formal arrest rate will increase, for instance, if the store

management becomes worried about the problem of inventory shrinkage and adopts a "get tough" policy for a
period of time. There are also variations between stores.
Store officials differ in the proportion of persons they feel
it desirable to charge formally. "Sheer caprice" may play a
part. Since knowledge of prosecution policy is not something store officials desire to make public, they discuss the
problems involved with an outsider only with the understanding that they will not be quoted. Enough information
was gathered in interviews with protection officials of stores
in several cities, however, to make it seem likely that,
among department stores, "class" stores generally prefer
charges against a smaller proportion of arrested persons
than do "mass" stores. Store detectives who have worked
in both types of stores agreed with this generalization.
Prosecution policy of "mass" stores requires less emphasis
on screening. Persons who shoplift in "mass" stores are already somewhat self-selected for lower social class status,
and the likelihood of a prominent individual or his wife
entering a "not guilty" plea and being found so by the
court is therefore not as great as in the "class" stores.

Aside from the circumstances influencing the arrest records of the Chicago "loop" department stores generally,
there may also be special circumstances affecting only the
arrests of the particular store studied here, the Lakeside Co.
The biases were not introduced by the research process of
this study since the sample of arrests by the store used in
the study includes every fourth arrest for shoplifting selected chronologically by order of arrest from the files of
the Lakeside Co. retail store in the Chicago "loop." (The
arrest records used here do not include those of surburban
stores.) The sample omits no case for any reason. In all,

1153 arrests make up the sample. But how adequate is this sample as a sample of all department store arrests?

The store is one of the largest in the city. It attempts to appeal, in its advertising, to all social classes of customers and it carries a wide price range of merchandise in departments from the crowded "Budget Floor," ("store-ese" for bargain basement) to the exclusive "Paris Shop" where elevators carry patrons to cocktails and hors d'oeuvres in the lounge while mink coats and Paris originals are being exhibited in the "little rooms" and the Grand Salon.

Inexpensive though some of its price lines may be, Lakeside Co. has, along with two or three other department stores in Chicago, a reputation for better goods and higher prices than most other stores. It is difficult to evaluate the influence of this "class" angle of the store on the social class distribution of its shoplifters. There is reason to believe (and it is the belief also of store detectives) that the "class" angle of the store does not exert much inhibiting influence on lower-class shoplifters. Shoplifters are, after all, *not* shoppers. They are in the store to steal rather than purchase merchandise. Only about 5 per cent to 10 per cent of shoplifters, and estimates vary within approximately this range, have with them at the time of their arrest items of merchandise for which they have sales receipts and which did not seem to be purchased merely for cover (a shoplifter may buy an inexpensive hat which she immediately "exchanges" for an expensive one). Pilferers from less opulent economic backgrounds need not feel conspicuous even in more elite sections of the store since they can generally dress rather well; some or many of their merchandise needs have been met outside their budgets through what juvenile pilferers refer to as the "five finger discount."

Thus there is no good economic reason why most shoplifters should not obtain merchandise in whatever store
they prefer.

In a later section of this study the possible class relationship of the Lakeside Co. shoplifters and shoppers will
be discussed (a considerable amount of occupational and
residential data was found on the question). It seems most
likely, however, that just as there is a wide range of goods
to buy so there is a wide range of goods to steal. No shoplifter would feel that stealing at Lakeside Co. was beneath
him socially (although the more successful commercial
shoplifters, as one of them declared, wouldn't be "caught
dead" in the basement store). Thus in terms of social class,
Lakeside Co. arrest data are probably more representative
of shoplifters in the "loop" than in most other stores.
When rich people want to shoplift in Chicago, they may
well shoplift at Lakeside Co., but so will poor people.

One possible distortion for the Lakeside Co. records
probably results from the fact that it is a well-policed store.
Among shoplifters who are "in the know," and these are
primarily the commercial thieves, the store is considered
to be a very unhealthy place in which to "work." For this
reason the proportion of commercial shoplifters is probably
lower than in some other stores.

The sex ratio of Lakeside Co. arrests is conditioned by
the fact that, while there is a large "men's store," the
largest number of people in the store, as in most downtown
department stores in any city, are adult women, apparently
middle class, relatively well-dressed, and middle-aged.

CHAPTER II

SHOPLIFTING

Arts and Crafts

THE TREATMENT of apprehended shoplifters differs in different types of stores, and so, to a degree, do the patterns of shoplifting. In part, grocery, book, drug, and hardware stores can afford to handle their shoplifters rather lightly because these stores do not usually carry on open display the types of merchandise attractive to most commercial shoplifters. Department stores, however, attract professionals and every arrested person must be regarded by store detectives as a possible professional shoplifter until he is shown to be otherwise.

In respect to the patterns of theft, shoplifters can be classified into two main groups on the basis of the use they make of stolen merchandise. *Commercial shoplifters,* "boosters," are those who steal merchandise to sell it. *Pilferers,* "snitches," steal merchandise for their own consumption. (Or, more succinctly, the booster steals for profit, the snitch steals for use.) The distinction between commercial shoplifting and pilfering is somewhat similar

39

to the distinction Jerome Hall has made between the
"professional" and the "lay" receiver of stolen property.
He differentiates them as follow:

1. The professional receiver *buys for the purpose of resale*,
   whereas the lay receiver buys for consumption.
2. Hence the professional receiver *sells* stolen merchandise,
   whereas the lay receiver *consumes* the goods.
3. The professional receiver *operates a business;* he deals in
   stolen commodities and is apt to be *in possession of a relatively large amount of such commodities, derived from
   different thefts and thieves,* as a stock in trade; the lay
   receiver does not operate a business nor does he deal in or
   possess a large quantity of stolen commodities.[1]

Professional thieves, with a finer discernment of grada-
tions in their own ranks, divide commercial shoplifters
into "heels" and "boosters." Heels are professional shoplifters who are rarely involved in other forms of crime.
They do not usually turn from shoplifting to pocket picking or to robbery. One might say that they are specialists in
crime and not general practitioners. "Ordinary" boosters,
on the other hand, are in fairly large proportion involved
in narcotics addiction, alcoholism, or prostitution. They
engage in shoplifting as one of many forms of illegal activity. The term "booster" is loosely and generally used to
cover all professional thieves who shoplift, whether specialists or not, and it is so used in the title of this book.

The pilferers form the largest body of shoplifters. They
appear to be chronic thieves, shoplifting with some frequency and regularity. There may also be in their ranks a few
impulsive persons who steal an occasional item of merchan-

1. Hall, Jerome. *Theft, Law, and Society.* (Indianapolis, 1952), p.
291.

dise. But most pilferers enter the store with intent to steal. The frequent assertion of the arrested person that the theft was a unique experience is doubted by experienced store detectives. Search of the self-professed "unique" thief, indeed, usually reveals other stolen merchandise.

Store detectives comment that people who enter a store to purchase merchandise rather than to steal it do not switch in midstream. They see many instances of frustrated shoppers who cannot find a sales clerk to wait on them, or even cashiers to take their money, but such shoppers, no matter how angry, do not walk off with the merchandise; they return it to a shelf; although seldom to the shelf on which it belongs.

While observing through a "one way" mirror a display of gift merchandise during the pre-Christmas season, a store detective and I spent many days of "fruitless" observation. The set-up was such as to lead the customers to believe themselves to be unobserved. The tables on which merchandise was lavishly and attractively displayed were partitioned on three sides into relatively small sections. That the customers really thought they were unobserved was, moreover, evidenced by their behavior. Women glanced furtively around and then pulled downward on girdles. Men adjust underclothing also, and both men and women occasionally thrust their faces into the mirrors (sometimes within inches of my face) and removed false teeth for on-the-spot relief and repair.

Throughout the ten-day period of observation no one stole anything. Customers, distressed because they could not find sales clerks to take their money, sometimes put merchandise back on the nearest table and left in an obvious "huff." Other customers would wait impatiently and angrily, or with experienced resignation, until one of the overburdened sales staff could be summoned to attend them. Both the store detective and I agreed (in whispered conversation) that if ever shoplifting could be a justifiable offense, this was the time. "Take them for goodness sake, and go," the detective once muttered as an aside to me after having seen a women holding a pair of candlesticks in one hand for twenty minutes and a five dollar bill in the other.

However, to repeat, neither of us observed anyone stealing anything. The comments of store detectives were, in this instance, confirmed. People who come into the store to buy, buy if they can. The thought of stealing does not occur to the legitimate customer, or, if it does, it is immediately rejected. Shoplifters, on the other hand, come into the store to steal prepared with their personal rationalizations as well as, frequently, with the physical evidence of illegal intent.

Professional Shoplifters: According to a member of the Chicago Police Department shoplifting detail, there are only a few genuinely professional shoplifters who make Chicago the headquarters of their operation. New York is rumored to have a good many more. The reason for the difference, the police believe, is that professionals prefer to work a large number of small stores rather than a few large ones because the professionals soon become known to store detectives. Chicago does not begin to approach New York in the number and variety of small stores carrying the good quality of merchandise the booster prefers.

At this point it may be well to introduce a small glossary of terms which is part of the argot of commercial shoplifters and thieves in general.

Heel: a real "professional" commercial shoplifter.

Booster: any commercial shoplifter or any thief who turns to shoplifting intending to sell the merchandise he steals.

Snitch: thieves' argot for a pilferer.

Clout (verb or noun): to shoplift; one who is engaged in the act of shoplifting.

Bennywork: clouting under the protection of an overcoat.

Pennyweighter: jewel thief.

Skin worker: fur thief.

Crotch worker: a booster who has trained herself to hold merchandise beneath her dress and between her legs and walk out of the store.

Cover, shade, stall (verb or noun): to act as an accomplice to the clout.

Hustle, put his back up, secure, set up, throw a hump: to distract the attention of a sales person or store detective (also used by pickpockets who likewise wish to distract the victim).

Booster skirt or bloomers, pants, coat, apron: garments especially designed to hold stolen merchandise.

Booster box: a garment box or other box designed in advance by the booster to look like a wrapped package but with an opening into which articles may be placed.

Store detectives also use the term "bad bag," meaning a paper bag with the store imprint which has been folded and unfolded numerous times indicating that the shoplifter has used it many times to conceal merchandise. A survey of several hundred shoplifters arrested in one store indicated about 20 per cent of them carried "bad bags."[2]

Items of trade equipment often found in the possession of both boosters and practiced snitches are manicure scis-

2. For much of this glossary of terms the author is indebted to Loren Edwards. (*Shoplifting and Shrinkage Protection for Stores.* [Springfield, Ill., 1958.])

sors or a razor blade plus a wooden match—to remove price tags. The razor blade is a form of disposable knife. Held between the second and third fingers with the match thrust through the opening in the blade for support, it can readily be used to remove price tags and labels and, when need be, inconspicuously discarded—even flushed down the toilet in the rest room along with other incriminating evidence. The razor blade is also used by pickpockets and purse snatchers ("moll-buzzers"). The old "pros" among pickpockets who can "reef" a wallet (i.e., pinch the pocket to force the wallet upward) take a dim view of the newer (and cruder) generation who use a razor blade to cut the pocket open on one side and remove the wallet. Women's purses are easily stolen by slashing the purse handle and the theft may be temporarily undetected if the woman has other bundles on the same arm.

"Heels" sometimes work alone but often they work in "troupes," sometimes touring the country and staying only long enough in any one town to "clout" and perhaps market merchandise. Sometimes the troupe is quite large: a West Coast troupe described by the head of the protection department of a nationwide chain of department stores, consisted of twelve to fifteen members. They specialized in entering stores at about lunch hour. Two "stalls" would "throw a hump," which brought the store detectives to one spot and attracted the attention of the remaining salesclerks. While this disturbance progressed, about a dozen "clouts" "cleaned" the rest of the store as thoroughly as their capacity to carry merchandise permitted. This troupe not only took display merchandise but stole "understock" as well, leaving whole shelves completely bare. But such large-scale enterprise is unusual. One stall, one clout, and perhaps a cover to take the goods from the clout or to conceal the clout's exit is the more usual pattern for professional troupes.

Fundamentally the troupe's plan of action is simple. Any of the time-honored devices to divert attention can be used. A simulated faint or heart attack, a small fire, etc., will give the clout the time he needs to conceal the pre-selected merchandise or to pass it on to the "cover." Since there is little risk that the merchandise will immediately be missed, the troupe can make a leisurely exit. An entire operation takes but a few minutes, and a troupe can clout several stores in a single day.

Most professional shoplifters work in small troupes but a few prefer to work alone. One "well-respected" professional said that she had never experienced any need for a stall. She cleared the ground for herself by acting the part of a disagreeable, fussy, bargain-hunting shopper. Consequently, sales clerks who knew her type vanished on seeing her. Furthermore, she changed her dress and hair-do frequently and tried never to steal the same merchandise two times in exactly the same way. Her disagreeability as well as her ability to alter her appearance, the store detectives agreed, was a major factor in her success. A detective told of once seeing her in the store. Her appearance was different enough from her appearance on previous occasions that the detective could not be certain of identification (for a known shoplifter loitering in a store may be arrested on sight under certain circumstances). Anxious to arrest her quickly the detective allowed the suspect to precede her half way up the escalator, then called out her name in a loud friendly way. The shoplifter turned around and was soon off on another trip to the lockup, cursing herself and laughing somewhat sourly with the store detective at the same time.

One very short woman who operated in Chicago for a time, but later appeared to have vanished from the city, stole nothing but ladies' suits. Her small size made it possible for her to conceal herself behind clothing racks, which are about five feet high. About half an hour before closing time in the store, she selected the merchandise to be taken and firmly pinned the skirts and jackets she had selected to the hangers so they would not drop off in transit. Then just at the closing hour she returned to the selected merchandise and put the suits (hangers and all) inside her bulky coat and left the store with the lingering crowd of shoppers. The final operation of stealing the merchandise took only seconds to complete and was done so adroitly that store detectives watched her on three occasions before they were finally sure that she was a thief.

A man "professional" who specialized in men's suits always hung the suits—and he took four or five at a time—from a chain he wore around his neck for the purpose, and his overcoat was especially tailored to conceal the merchandise hanging underneath it. Another man worked with lined trousers. Store detectives say that they have picked him up leaving the store with so much merchandise stuffed between the trouser and the lining that he was barely able to walk.

"Booster skirts" or bloomers are occasionally used by women. The booster skirt may be designed in any manner consistent with the current fashion; even the sheath dress may be adapted to conceal merchandise in a hammock-like bag suspended between the legs. A full skirt with an elastic waist band, however, is most convenient and a shoplifter wearing a booster skirt can acquire the appearance of advanced pregnancy. If the store detective has not noted the rapidity with which the pregnancy symptoms have developed, he may be the more reluctant to arrest the shoplifter.

Booster bloomers (old fashioned bloomers with double rows of tight elastic at the knees) can be worn under booster skirts. Slits or pockets in the skirt or dress or an elastic waistband allow merchandise to be stuffed into the concealing recesses of the bloomers. Coat linings tailored to hold merchandise inserted through openings in the bottom of the pockets can be adapted by either men or women. A large handbag, brief case, or shopping bag (often a "bad bag") is usually the trademark of the sophisticated shoplifter, whether booster or snitch.

Booster boxes can be most ingeniously designed to hold whatever kind of merchandise the specialist-shoplifter has predetermined he will steal. To the observer the box will perhaps appear to be a package prepared for mailing, but the addition of a slot in the side or bottom can allow the shoplifter to insert, for example, ten or a dozen LP records without unwrapping the box. Similar boxes or brief cases with hinged side or bottom openings held together by springs on the inside can be used for shirts, sweaters, neckties, or even portable typewriters in cases. Shoplifters can be as versatile and ingenious as professional package designers.

Even perfect technique fails occasionally, but the advantage the professional shoplifter has (as with most professional thieves) over other shoplifters is his ability to use influence and "know-how" in resolving his case without a lengthy jail or prison sentence. An attorney will have been carefully selected for his "right" connections (a condition rumored not to be too difficult to ascertain in many municipal courts).

Apparent privilege in the court for an arrested commercial shoplifter is a matter on which it is difficult for the research worker to comment except in a general way. However, one instance was directly observed in which a shoplifter was found "guilty" and fined $25.00 by the judge; the prosecuting attorney reported that the shoplifter had no prior criminal record. I had been advised by private detectives to visit the court and see the proceedings since, in fact, the defendant had been arrested and found guilty in that court at least nine times. The judge, prosecuting attorney, and court social worker recognized the defendant and addressed him by his first name. But for the record, it was stated by the prosecutor that he was a first offender. Speaking with the shoplifter after the trial (having been introduced to him by a store detective), this professional shoplifter stated that he paid his lawyer a "regular retainer" and that the fee was worth the cost. The well-known "fix" was in operation, but the shoplifter complained it was relatively expensive. The attorney had been forced to ask for three continuances of the case until the right judge was on the bench and the right man from the prosecuting attorney's office would be the prosecutor in court on the day of the trial. Of two other well-known professional shoplifters whose records were checked, one had never received more than a $25.00 fine and had been discharged or given a token sentence ($1.00 considered paid, and one day considered served) a total of twelve times. The other had once been given six months probation and once fined $50.00. Other numerous arrests known to store detectives had taken place (she had a total of seven aliases under which she had been arrested and charged by one department store alone); these did not appear in her police record. The cards recording these arrests must have been lifted—a part of the "fix" procedure.

Boosters: Similar to the specialist professional shoplifters (heels) in having easily identifiable criminal connections and in purloining mainly salable merchandise is the non-specialist group of boosters. In part, this category is composed of alcoholics and narcotics addicts for whom shoplifting is one way of picking up a few desperately needed dollars. The "frantic addict" with no money to pay for his drug who dashes into a department store and grabs merchandise ("clouts and lams") is a well-known phenomenon in store life. He comes to the attention of store detectives rather frequently since he is often in haste and lacks the finesse or the troupe support of the real professional. Since he is often turned over to the police for possessing narcotics ("booked" on a narcotics charge rather than on shoplifting), he does not always appear in shoplifting records. However, aside from alcoholics and narcotics addicts with well-defined criminal associations, there is a considerable number of career thieves who turn from shoplifting to check forging, confidence games, etc., and back again. In Sutherland's *Professional Thief*, Chick Conwell, who was primarily a pickpocket, describes one exciting shoplifting tour in which he stole a valuable scarf, stuffing it into a brief case.[3] Among the total group of shoplifters considered in the present study were several men who at one time or another had been arrested for burglary, auto larceny, armed robbery, assault with a deadly weapon,

3. Sutherland, Edwin H. *The Professional Thief*. (Chicago, 1937) p. 40–41.

carrying concealed weapons, and even several who were subsequently (and one who had been previously) arrested for murder. These people were not professional shoplifters. The true professionals look down on armed robbers and other criminals who happen to shoplift once in a while as an easy way of turning a dishonest dollar.

HISTORY OF SHOPLIFTING

The history of crime shows that professional shoplifting is an ancient if not honorable art, and the techniques of operation seem to have changed relatively little through the centuries. Until the advent of mass-produced, ready-made clothing, toys, cameras, radios, and household gadgets, thieves apparently concentrated largely on stealing silks, velvets, and silver. One of the earliest known accounts of shoplifting, written in 1597, describes a professional troupe consisting of a "clout" and two "covers." Only the language and argot, but not the technique of operation, differentiates this from a modern description.

The higher degrees and gentlemen-lifts have to the performance of their faculty three parties of necessity, the lift, the marker, and the santar. The lift, attired in the form of a civil country gentlemen, comes with the marker into some mercer's shop, haberdasher's, goldsmith's, or any such place where any particular parcels of worth are to be conveyed, and there he calls to see a bolt of satin, velvet, or any such commodity, and, not likeing the pile, colour, or brack, he calls for more, and whiles he begins to resolve which of them most fitly may be lifted, and what garbage (for so he calls the goods stolen) may be most easily conveyed. Then he calls to the mercer's man and says, "Sirrah, reach me that piece of velvet or satin, or that jewel, chain, or piece of plate"; and whilst the fellow turns his back, he commits his garbage to the marker; for note the lift is without his cloak, in his doublet and hose, to avoid the more suspicion: The marker, which is the receiver of the lift's luggage, gives a wink to the santar, that walks before the window, and then, then santar going by in great haste, the marker calls to him and says, "Sir, a word with you. I have a message to do unto you from a friend of yours, and the errand is of some importance."

"Truly sir," says the santar, "I have urgent business in hand, and as at this time I cannot stay."

"But one word, and no more," says the marker, and then he delivers to him whatsoever the lift has conveyed to him; and then the santar goes on his way, who never came within the shop, and is a man unknown to them all.[4]

One hundred years later (1726) the techniques of theft and the kinds of merchandise taken were similar, but the problem of the professional shoplifter had apparently become more acute to merchants. In *The Lives of Remarkable Criminals* is described a "troupe" consisting of Jane Holmes, "the woman Burton," and Mary Robinson. The three "fenced" their merchandise through the notorious "thief taker," Jonathan Wild. They were apprehended in the best modern manner.

In the summer of the year 1726, shoplifters became so common, and so detrimental to the shopkeepers, that they made application to the Government for assistance in apprehending the offenders; and in order there to, offered a reward and a pardon for any who would discover their associates in such practice.[5]

A stool pigeon, "the woman Burton" responded to the offer and informed on her associates Jane Holmes and Mary

4. Judges, A. F. *The Elizabethan Underworld.* (London, 1930), p. 170.

5. Hayward, Arthur L. (ed). *Lives of the Most Remarkable Criminals.* (London, 1735), p. 375.

Robinson and their fence, Jonathan Wild. The three were apprehended, tried, and *executed* for their crimes.

Jane Holmes, of good family, came up to London from the country when she was sixteen. She married a "sharp" trader who subsequently left her. She then took to shoplifting and apparently practiced it quite successfully for many years although she denied some of the crimes attributed to her by Burton. She was arrested and found guilty of stealing

some twenty yards of straw-ground brocaded silks value £10, the goods of John Moon and Richard Stone, on the first of June, 1726; of stealing, in the shop of Mr. Mather Herbert, forty yards of pink-coloured mantua silk, value £10, on the first of May, in the same year; of stealing in company with Mary Robinson, a silver cup of the value of £5, the goods of Elizabeth Dobbenson, on the seventh January; of stealing, in company of Mary Robinson afore-said, eighty yards of cherry-coloured mantua silk value £5, the goods of Joseph Bourn, and Mary Harper, on the twenty-forth of December.[6]

She was executed at Tyburn. Of Mary Robinson, her companion, the author says:

The indescretions of youth are always to be pittied, and often excused even by those who suffer most from them: but when persons grown up to years of discretion continue to pursue with eagerness the most flagitious courses, and grow in wickedness as they grow in age, pity naturally forsakes us, and they appear in so exercable a light that instead of having compassion for their misfortune we congratulate our country on being rid of such monsters, whom nothing could tame, nor the approach even of death in a natural way hinder them from anticipating it by drawing on a violent one through their crimes.

I am drawn to this observation from the fate of the miserable

6. *Ibid.*, p. 376.

woman of whom we are now speaking. What her parents were or what her education it is impossible to say, since she was shy of relating them herself; and being 70 years old at the time of her execution, there was nobody then living who could give an account of her. She was indicted for stealing a silver cup in company with Jane Holmes, the property of Joseph Brown and Mary Harper, on the 24th day of December. On these facts she was convicted as the rest were, in the evidence of Burton, who, as is usual in such cases, they represented as a woman worse than themselves, who had drawn many of them into the commission of which she now deposed against them.

As to the old woman Mary Robinson, she said she had been a widow 14 years, and had both children and grandchildren living at the time of her execution; she said she had worked as hard for her living as any woman in London. Yet when pressed thereupon to speak the truth and not wrong her concience in the last moments, she did then declair that she had been guilty of thieving tricks. . . .

Possibly my readers may wonder how such a large quantity of silks were conveyed away. I think therefore proper to inform them that in the evidence Burton said they had a contrivance under petticoats not unlike two large hooks, upon which they laid a whole roll of silk, and so conveyed it away at once, while one of the company amused the people of the shop in some manner or other until they got out of reach; and by this means they had for many years carried on together their trade with great success and as much safety, until the losses of the tradesmen ran so high as to induce them to take the method aforementioned, and quickly produced a discovery, not only of the persons of the offenders, but of the place also where they had deposited the goods.[7]

A typical shoplifting troupe operating in the 1870's in America is described by Phillip Farley in his *Criminals of America; or Tales of the Lives of Thieves Enabling Everyone to be his own Detective*:

7. *Ibid.*, p. 376.

Young ladies, and frequently young men, under certain and very agreeable circumstances, have a forcible way of putting it, and "two are company, and three are none." Shoplifters reverse the order of that, and believe in three for company. . . . The company usually consists of a man and two women. They dress well, and might readily be taken for people in an easy way of life.

On entering a store . . . the man does the opening part of the conversation. He endeavors to concentrate the salesman's mind, who advances to attend the "customers," on the extent of the purchases they are going to make. As they talk, they move to the particular part of the store where the goods they ask for are sold. Then the first woman concentrates her powers on the salesman. During this the second one strolls around and studies the situation. The moment she feels secure from observation, she sets to work, filling a large bag attached to her waist by a strong cord and when she gets all she can carry, joins the others. This bag hangs in front under the dress, and has the opening large enough to admit easily an entire piece of silk.

On coming up to her companions, she becomes interested in the purchase they are making, and for a minute or two they remain together to ward off suspicion.

An excuse is then made, and the three leave the establishment.[8]

In 1886 Inspector Thomas Byrnes in his *Professional Criminals of America*, noted, possibly for the first time in popular print, the existence of the noncommercial shoplifter referred to as the "kleptomaniac" noting that the word had a special meaning in regard to shoplifting.

There are generally two classes of shoplifters—the regular criminal professional and the kleptomaniac. The very poor classes seldom take a hand in it. Poverty is held by the world to be the badge of crime, and the poor slattern who enters a store is sure to be so carefully watched that larceny is next to

8. Farley, Phillip. *Criminals of America.* (New York, 1876), pp. 53–54.

impossible. [A situation not so very different from that prevailing in stores today and discussed again in a later chapter.]

The shoplifter is always a person of fair appeal and she generally has a comfortable home. If she be a professional she may be one of a criminal community and her home may be shared by some other engaged in equally evil ways. If she be a kleptomaniac—and in shoplifting the word has peculiar significance—she is possibly a woman whose life in other respects is exemplary. It does seem strange that a wife and mother whose home is an honest one, who attends religious services regularly, and who seems far removed from the world of crime, should be so carried away by her admiration of some trinket or knicknack as to risk her home, honor, and everything to secure it. But the annals of metropolitan offenses are full of instances of just this kind. It is the sexes fondness for finery that nine times out of ten gets them into trouble.[9]

Describing professional shoplifters, Inspector Thomas Byrnes wrote:

Two or three shoplifters have been known to enter large cloth dry goods or ostrich feather establishments in the morning just before business opening time, and while a porter or clerk was sweeping out. On some pretext or another one of the rogues engages the single guardian of the store in conversation, and invariably succeeds in luring the unsuspecting man to the rear of the place. This is the thieves' opportunity, and when the porter's or clerk's back is turned to them the shoplifters confederates are busy. In a twinkling they conceal whatever goods they are able to capture in false pockets upon their person. Then the first man tells his dupe that he will call again, and leaves the store after his associates.[10]

Benjamin Eldridge, writing also in the United States, noted in 1890 that "the regular or professional 'shoplifter'

9. Byrnes, Thomas F. *Professional Criminals of America.* (New York, 1886), pp. 31–32.
10. *Ibid.*, p. 33.

is to be distinguished from the amateurs who occasionally yield to temptation. . . ."[11] He also pictures the operation of a professional troupe:

As a matter of fact the women shoplifters probably outnumber the men and the reason is apparent in the better facility for concealment of stolen goods which a woman's dress secures. Large bags for holding plunder of every description are sometimes artfully draped and fastened under the skirt of a dress or the back of a cloak. This is technically known as the shoplifter's "kick," and experience perfected an improvement in this device in the form of the "hoisting kick" or short overskirt covering an ordinary dress skirt so stitched that the lining and the skirt make a complete bag around the body from the waist to the heels. This bag was often packed full of articles, slipped into it through a slit concealed by the apron overskirt. One notorious shop-lifter was caught no long ago in the act of stealing a cake of scented soap. Upon examination sixteen yards of silk, fifty yards of lace, two pairs of silk stockings, one silk and one lace handkerchief, and a scarf pin were extracted from her clothing.[12]

Professional shoplifters and boosters of all varieties constitute a *minority* of arrests for shoplifting. Store detectives agree that not over 10 per cent of the shoplifters in any department store are stealing in order to market the stolen merchandise. (This figure would not necessarily hold for camera or similar stores.) The value of the merchandise "boosters" steal is, of course, much greater than the proportion of their numbers, and from the victim's point of view detecting professionals and keeping them out of the store is perhaps the most important task of the protection staff. During the year one man professional was in prison

11. Eldridge, Benjamin and Wm. B. Watts. *Our Rival the Rascal.* (Boston, 1897), pp. 29–30.
12. *Ibid.*, p. 31.

on a grand larceny charge, for example, the inventory shrinkage in the men's suit department of one store alone was reduced by $4,000.

The differentiation between the booster and the heel is often merely one of specialization. Compared with "con" men and well-protected racketeers, both are of low social prestige in the criminal world. Fundamentally, although differing in technique and finesse, both heels and boosters steal merchandise and sell or pawn it. The value they receive for stolen merchandise is usually about one-third of the price tag value.

Their "outlets" for sales of stolen merchandise include, of course, the modern version of the "fence" or "thief taker" of Jonathan Wild's day, but commercial thieves are not limited to selling through "fences." Store protection officials of large retail stores believe that only a minority of commercial thieves market their stolen merchandise through recognized criminal channels. Most commercial shoplifters, they have reason to suspect, furnish supplies to small retail specialty shops which function as, and perhaps are, in the main, legitimate retail stores. The security official of a large chain of retail stores selling books and art supplies said that he was preparing legal cases against a small neighborhood store whose proprietor was knowingly buying stolen merchandise. "It works like this," he said, "a man comes into a neighborhood store with a lot of expensive books and equipment in his car. They're worth maybe $800–900 wholesale. He says he's just closed up his store in Philadelphia. He's willing to sell the left-over stock for what he can get out of it. The proprietor doesn't ask any questions but shells out maybe $200–300 for the lot. He even gets a sales receipt signed with some phony

name. He knows he's buying 'hot goods,' but he thinks
he's covered the legal side and stands to make a nice
profit. He won't sell the stuff to just anybody, but he has
some good customers he's known for a long time. They'll
be glad to be let in on a bargain, and they won't ask any
questions."

Photographic supply store owners, jewelers, neighborhood women's and men's wear stores, electrical appliance
shops, and the like are also suspected of acquiring considerable proportions of their stock in implicit collusion
with people they actually know to be thieves. Needless
to say, legal proof of "knowingly receiving stolen property"
is very difficult, and the small time "wheeler-dealer" retail
merchant may not be able to operate at all if he observes
conscientiously all of the legal requirements of his trade.

No special effort has been made in this study to go into
the potentially available sources of knowledge of the habits
and backgrounds of commercial shoplifters. Heels and
boosters are apparently not different from others who earn
their living by theft. Analysis of their behavior patterns as
revealed by the limited data of this study would probably
add relatively little information to the understanding of
criminal behavior, for many studies have been made of
professional thieves.

Pilferers: Only about 10 per cent of arrested department
store shoplifters are thieves who steal merchandise as one
way of making a living. The other 90 per cent are—in
thieves argot—the "snitches." The snitch is usually a respectable person. He does not think of himself as a snitch.
In fact, he has probably never heard the word. But nevertheless he is a shoplifter. The composite picture that
emerges from this study is one of the chronic pilferer as

a systematic thief stealing merchandise for his own use. Normally he has no criminal associations or connections; yet he (in department stores, most often she) comes into the store usually equipped with a large handbag, brief case, shopping bag, "bad bag," or sometimes even booster bloomers or a booster bag in which to carry off merchandise. She may have scissors or a razor blade to snip off price tags. She deliberately directs the sales clerk's attention elsewhere and slips various items into her bag when she believes herself unobserved. She may even bring with her a shopping list of items she wants to steal. Looking for such "shoplifting lists" is routine for store detectives. Having acquired a portion of her loot, she may go to a store rest room and flush price tags and other incriminating evidence down the toilet. She will wear as much as is possible of her recently stolen merchandise in order to lighten her load and then proceed to stash away the rest. Her loot at the end of the day may range from one to thirty pieces of merchandise. She does not make many legitimate purchases; although it is probable that most snitches do buy their largest pieces of clothing such as coats and suits and confine their snitching to smaller and more easily concealed objects. The snitches, that is to say, are not impulsive, erratic individuals suddenly "taken" with an uncontrollable urge for a pretty bauble. They are deliberate thieves who manifest intent to steal by preparation beforehand and who carry out their crimes with system and method. They are sufficiently practiced that only by considerable interrogation can they be differentiated professional thieves. Although they are, as we shall see, almost always technically "first offenders" when apprehended by store police, their behavior indicates only that they have not been *caught* before; it does not indicate that they have not previously shoplifted—quite the contrary.

Because of the selective screening procedures of the store detectives, pilferers appear in official police arrest statistics much less frequently than in store statistics. But statistics resulting from "accidents" of the administrative action of the private police, public police, and courts cannot form the basis for a social-psychological theory. Although reported privately rather than publicly, pilfering is still criminal behavior.

CHAPTER III

PRIVATE POLICE
AND UNREPORTED CRIME

The Problem of the Missing Data

ONLY ONE PHASE of the problem of unreported crime will be presented in this work: *shoplifting, defined as theft from a retail store by people who pose as legitimate customers of the store.* Shoplifting, although a major source of unreported criminal statistics, is but one crime among many which must be studied before the work of private police can be charted; and the operation of private police represents a challenging problem in the field of criminology.

If law violators (shoplifters and others) apprehended by private police were generally prosecuted in the courts, they would not constitute the problem for criminological theory which they do now. The crimes and criminals would then be part of the public record, and data recorded about them would be available to research workers in sociology and psychology. But this is not so because in a large proportion of cases the victims of the crimes do not wish to prosecute the thieves in court. Many victims of embezzlement, "till tapping," larceny, and fraud agree to withhold prosecution if the thief will make restitution of some or all of the stolen money or merchandise, and restitution is often more satisfactory to the victim than imprisonment of the offender. Restitution may also be a more satisfactory "out" for the criminal.

The existence of persons apprehended committing crimes but not prosecuted in the courts is in one respect analogous to the "white collar crime" pointed out by Edwin H. Sutherland in 1940[1] when he posited the need for a thoroughgoing re-evaluation of the then current theories of crime because these theories had been based on samples of criminals who were prosecuted only through the efforts of public police. The data on which theories of crime causation had been based, Sutherland showed, omitted the records of government commissions and investigative agencies. Concerning theories of crime causation, Sutherland wrote:

The conventional explanations are invalid principally because they are derived from biased samples. The samples are biased in that they have not included vast areas of criminal behavior of persons not in the lower class. One of these neglected areas is the criminal behavior of business and professional men.[2] [Italics added, M.O.C.]

In the ensuing twenty-four years, theories of crime causation have been somewhat modified in recognition of the importance of the body of data which Sutherland called "white collar crime." The tendency, however, has been for writers in the field of criminology to distort

1. "White Collar Criminality," *American Sociological Review.* February, 1940.
2. *Ibid.*

Sutherland's hypothesis and to present crime as character-istic of social extremes. Big businessmen commit crimes (of some kinds) and slum dwellers commit crimes (of other kinds). The middle classes continue, in assumption at least, to be relatively virtuous, respectable, clinging to their crime-free "middle-class values."

In addition to the "ordinary" crimes reported to the po-lice, Sutherland added the white collar crimes uncovered by investigating boards and commissions. In the records of private police, however, there is still another field of criminal behavior which must also be considered if our the-ories of crime causation are not to continue to be based on data unrepresentative of the whole range of crimes. The ex-tent of these crimes can only be inferred.

In New York City there are about 24,000 uniformed po-lice engaged in all types of prevention and detection of law violation including traffic violations. According to A. S. Taylor, Assistant Director of the Division of Licenses of the State of New York (December 11, 1958), there were 10,000 private police employed by 631 licensed private in-vestigative bureaus. Most of the private police are em-ployed in the prevention, investigation, and detection of crimes which never become part of public records. From the standpoint of the student of criminal behavior, private police records represent an untapped mine of information.[3]

Private police are employed in considerable number by business firms for the prevention of theft, the apprehension of thieves, and the detection of fraud, embezzlement, and

3. In 1933, J. P. Shalloo presented a picture of private police activity largely vis-a-vis labor interests. He also gave some fruitful hints about the kinds of crime and the extent of crime handled almost wholly by private police, but the hints appear never to have been followed up in research studies. "Private Police," *American Academy of Political and Social Science,* Monograph No. 1, 1933.

other crimes. They are regularly employed by department stores, loan companies, hotels, industrial plants, retail specialty and variety stores, banks, railways, trucking firms, and insurance companies. In fact, they are employed in most commercial enterprises in which valuable equipment or merchandise must be protected from theft, in which any considerable number of people handle other people's money, and in which relationships of trust must be established or employees bonded. Some private police are employed directly by businesses; others are employed by large agencies which contract services to businesses. The Burns Agency, Pinkerton, and Willmark are perhaps the best known, but several thousand national and local agencies exist in the country.

If, however, the law violators apprehended by private police are not prosecuted, can they still be considered criminal? Sutherland developed the thesis that "persons of the upper socio-economic class engage in much criminal behavior; that this criminal behavior differs from the criminal behavior of the lower socio-economic class principally in the administrative procedures which are used in dealing with offenders; and that variations in administrative procedures are not significant from the point of view of the causation of crime."[4]

This thesis has been widely accepted. If it is correct, then the fact that the victim does not report the crime to the public police but retains his own detection department or agency is also not significant from the point of view of the causation of crime. In other words, crime is crime whether judged so by official agencies or not.

Recently this thesis might appear to have been chal-

4. Sutherland, Edwin H. *White Collar Crime.* (New York, 1949), p. 9.

lenged, in part, by Cloward and Ohlin.[5] Early in their study, they state: *"The delinquent act, then is defined by two essential elements: it is behavior that violates basic norms of the society, and, when officially known, it evokes a judgment by agents of criminal justice that such norms have been violated?"* (Italics in original.) They set these two criteria to differentiate delinquent behavior from other deviant behavior, for example bad manners. But apparently they do not intend the second criterion to be applied rigidly for when they reach the discussion of "protected" rackets, and other crimes protected from official sanction by the activity of political machines,[6] they have no hesitation in calling these *crimes* although no official sanction is evoked against the participants. "Variations in administrative procedure" are, as Sutherland stated, "not significant from the point of view of the causation of crime."

By no means all of the distortions which have resulted from basing theory solely or almost solely on data in public records, and omitting crimes handled by private police, can at present be satisfactorily determined. Nevertheless, even according to present scattered evidence, three points can be established with relative certainty: the number of law violators is underestimated; the relative frequency of different forms of crime has been distorted; and these distortions lead to incorrect appraisals of the age, sex, race, and social class characteristics and attributes of the criminal population.

1. *Number of law violators.* Since the records of private police have not been made generally or easily available for research purposes (nor have many research workers asked

5. Cloward, R. A. and L. E. Ohlin. *Delinquency and Opportunity.* (New York, 1961), p. 3.
6. *Ibid.*, p. 204 ff.

for them), the number of crimes handled by private police can only be inferred. In 1958 in the State of New York, as has been noted, there were 631 licensed detective agencies, which employed approximately 10,000 employees. It is, of course, not legitimate to compare the number of private police and the number of public police as simple indicators of the number of crimes because, among other reasons, some of their functions differ. But the presence of 10,000 private police, most of whom are paid to protect property and to apprehend law violators in the State of New York alone, coupled with the fact that their efforts, even when successful, seldom become matters of public record, is certainly cause for reflection.

2. *Relative frequency of different forms of crime.* Embezzlement, fraud, and other forms of larceny, in addition to shoplifting, are certainly grossly under-represented in conventional criminal statistics, because these are the crimes which private police are most frequently employed to investigate. How often are employees apprehended stealing money, goods, or tools from their employers? How frequent are attempts to deceive insurance companies? How often do people run away to avoid paying installments on their cars? How frequently are bonding companies called upon to make good on their bonds? At present all we can say is that these crimes are obviously of major consequence and are so considered by the business firms who employ— nationally—a veritable army of detectives, fraud investigators, and "skip tracers."

Similar to crimes handled by private police in that they are unrecorded statistically are the crimes which are handled or should be handled (for most of them go undetected or officially unreported) by Better Business Bureaus and other similar organizations. While it is generally known through newspaper reports and becomes obvious in the experience of living in any metropolitan area that a considerable number of offenses (misrepresentation of merchandise or services) are committed by used car salesmen, radio and TV repairmen, opticians, plumbers, physicians, attorneys, drug firms, etc., the prevalent acceptance of *caveat emptor* metamorphoses these into quasi-crimes. That they are extremely frequent was pointed out by Sutherland who observed that an inquiry, "What are some of the 'crooked practices' in your business?" made of any skilled tradesman or professional person will bring a lengthy report on competitors' illegal practices. We have to recognize also that the responsibility for awareness and care on the part of a buyer that was perhaps proper in an earlier period of simple machines and processes that could easily be understood is now anachronistic in view of the highly complex state of technology, science, and the arts.

These crimes and violations of trust are similar to the crimes detected by private police in that they are seldom made matters of official police record.

3. *Personal characteristics of offenders.* The under-representation of larceny, embezzlement, and violations of trust in conventional criminal statistics means *ipso facto* an under-representation of the "respectable" middle class among the offenders. One must be at least fairly well established in a community to borrow money from a commercial loan company, to be employed in a bank or as a retail clerk, or even to buy expensive merchandise on the installment plan. Fraudulent claims against insurance companies are not easily attempted by people without "respectable" backgrounds.

The terms "middle class" or "respectable middle class" as they are here used are less a description of occupational roles than a statement of psychological and social affiliation and aspiration level. Without distortion of the delineation of middle class and its values so well set out by Albert K. Cohen,[7] the term "middle class" can be stretched to include members of the economic working class who subscribe to certain values and aspirations including savings, home ownership, college education and business or professional careers for their children, constructive use of leisure time, respect for property, cultivation of manners, courtesy, personableness, and the like. "Some of our best examples," says Cohen[8] "of 'middle-class culture' are to be found in the 'upwardly mobile' working-class families."

Furthermore, it is useful to look at the "respectable middle-class values" themselves as actual sources for criminal behavior and not confine our observations to criminal or delinquent "sub-cultures." Do not, for example, the values of the middle class contain the belief that it is better to steal from or to defraud an impersonal corporation or an unknown individual customer than it is to fail to provide one's self and family with the money or goods symbolic of middle-class status?

PRIVATE POLICE RECORDS

The fact that the work of private police has been largely overlooked by the sociologists does not mean that it is an "unknowable" field. Some private police keep detailed records of apprehension and disposition of cases. With

7. Cohen, A. K. *Delinquent Boys*, (New York, 1955), pp. 88–91.
8. *Ibid*. p. 94.

proper safeguards for anonymity, some of these records can be made available to the legitimate researcher. The records of any large detective agency, properly analysed, would make a most significant contribution to the study of delinquency and crime.

Stimulated by the relative scarcity of information in the literature of criminology on the functioning of private agencies of law enforcement, the writer approached the protection manager of a leading Chicago department store asking if such data as had been collected on shoplifting and shoplifters might be made available for statistical analysis. Store officials cooperated wholeheartedly with the project and lent every assistance consistent with protecting the anonymity of the store and of the people arrested in it.

In addition to the private records of the Store, some of the public records of prosecutions for shoplifting in the Chicago Municipal Court were examined. Police Department information on the prior criminal careers of some of the shoplifters who had been convicted in court was also studied.

The end product is a research report with two sides. On one side is a type-study of shoplifting; of the kinds and values of merchandise stolen; of the personal backgrounds of shoplifters. The other side is a limited analysis of the function of a private police agency. Since however neither private police data nor shoplifting has been studied by other sociologists, the results, although suggestive, are certainly not conclusive.

CHAPTER IV

WHAT'S MISSING FROM THE STORE?

IN THE CHAPTER following this, the focus of attention will be on the shoplifter; in this chapter the focus is on the offense. However, since any act of shoplifting, unlike many other forms of crime (burglary, vandalism, armed robbery, etc.) is usually known to have taken place only when the offender is apprehended, most of the information about the offense must be based on the evidence of merchandise taken by offenders who have been caught. This chapter will necessarily say something about offenders also.

As was pointed out in Chapter I, there are only two measures of the extent of shoplifting in addition to that derived from persons apprehended, namely *inventory shrinkage* and *spot checking,* and neither of them is at all accurate. Inventory shrinkage, as we have seen, unfortunately includes other losses as well as those which take place through shoplifting, and spot checking can only give a fragmented picture. (It can, however, be of practical value. One university book store in New York, for example, displayed fifteen copies of a current "best seller" and instructed the sales clerks to sell no books from that particular display but only from the "understock." At the end of one day, three books from the display were missing. The management therefore was encouraged to take somewhat better protective measures for the merchandise in the store.)

VALUE OF MERCHANDISE SHOPLIFTED

As revealed by the Store data,[1] the source closest to the actual offense, a single shoplifting tour for the "run of the mill" shoplifter is not highly remunerative. For all persons in the sample, juvenile as well as adult, the median value of merchandise recovered per arrested person was only $6.00. More, of course, may have been stolen than was recovered, for some stolen merchandise may have been passed on to confederates. Also when identification tags and labels had been removed from some stolen objects by the shoplifter prior to arrest, the merchandise could not be legally identified as stolen. But it seems unlikely that either of these activities would have been sufficient materially to alter the figure.

The *median* values of recovered merchandise for each age and sex groups were: women, $6.74; girls, $5.00; men, $8.30; boys, $3.71.

The *mean* values of merchandise recovered, however, for adults were considerably higher: women, $16.40 (2.4 times the median); girls, $8.06 (1.6 times the median); men,

1. For a fairly complete discussion of the actual data, see Appendix p. 193ff.

$28.36 (3.5 times the median); boys, $7.14 (1.9 times the median). The differences between the means and the medians for adults indicates the existence of much more remunerative theft by a small number of adults.

About 6 per cent of all persons arrested had with them stolen merchandise valued at more than $50.00. Two per cent had taken goods valued at $100.00 or more. These values, it should be noted, are the price tag values of the merchandise and were obtained from the private records of the Store.

It is important, however, to keep in mind that the shoplifting tours that resulted in arrest and thus make up these data, were, in considerable part, tours *interrupted* by arrest. Detectives do not necessarily wait for the shoplifters to finish all of the thefts they may have planned before arresting them. "Intent" to steal could, in Illinois, be shown by such behavior as deliberate concealment, removing identification labels, etc. Moreover, there is no information as to how often shoplifters steal. Those who take the most expensive merchandise, quite possibly steal most frequently and regularly. They probably are also those possessing the greatest skill and ability in avoiding detection.

The median values of stolen merchandise when classified by the age and sex of the offender show both range and variance. Fifty per cent or more of shoplifters at all age levels take items of relatively small value (Charts 1 and 2). Twenty-five per cent of male shoplifters, however, were apprehended with merchandise valued at $35.00 or more, and 25 per cent of female shoplifters were also involved in the theft of merchandise of relatively large total value.

The evidence on the age and sex distribution of persons

who engage in the most lucrative type of shoplifting (other information shows that they are "boosters" for the most part) may be inferred from the age and sex distribution of all arrested persons who had with them at the time of their arrest, merchandise valued at $20.00 or more (Chart 1).

Adult men constituted 17.2 per cent of all adult arrests and 25.6 per cent of all adults arrested who had merchandise valued at $20.00 or more. Men at all age levels up to 70 stole valuable merchandise in 30–40 per cent of these cases. Among women, the proportion apprehended with valuable articles increased until 40–50 years of age, then gradually decreased. Between 20 and 29 years of age 20.7 per cent of women had in their possession stolen merchandise valued at $20.00 or more, and between 40 and 49 years of age the proportion was 28 per cent. The critical ratio between these per cents was 1.6.

Chart 1
Per cent of arrested persons stealing merchandise valued at
$20.00 or more; by age and sex

(Lakeside Co. Data)

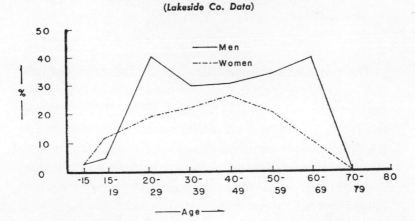

Chart 2
Per cent of arrested persons stealing merchandise valued at $5.00 or less; by age and sex

(Lakeside Co. Data)

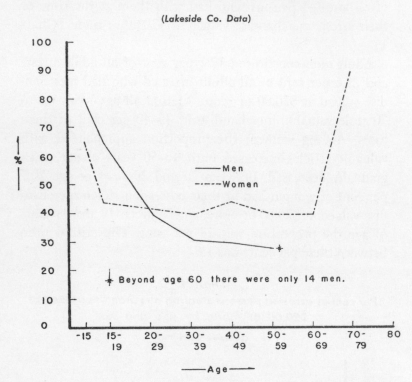

The procedure of calculating the critical ratio between two percentages is discussed at some length in *Psychological Statistics* by Quinn McNemar (pp. 62 ff). In general, the higher the critical ratio, the more certain one is that the difference between two sets of figures is a real difference and not just a happenstance in a particular set of statistics. A critical ratio of 3.0 or more implies (statistically we must always say, all things being equal) that the difference is real and significant and will be repeated whenever statistics are gathered. Smaller critical ratios imply that the magnitude of the difference may have been due to chance.

The formula used in computing the critical ratio of differences between two per cents was:

$$\frac{D}{\sigma \, p_1 - p_2}$$

$$\text{In which } \sigma \, p_1 - p_2 = \sqrt{\frac{p_1 q_1}{N_1} + \frac{p_2 q_2}{N_2}}$$

The critical ratio (C.R.) formula takes into account the number of people in two different groups and the magnitude of the difference found between them. The figure represents, thus, the simplest way of saying, "With the data collected for a sample of cases, the differences between two groups seem to be of this or that degree of importance." The degree is expressed by the C.R. Large differences between small groups of people and small differences between large numbers of people thus have a single figure which will accurately express their usefulness.

The number of men involved in stealing merchandise from the Store of over $20.00 value is too few (only 51) to make the age analysis of much significance, but men seem to have two peak ages; the first in the twenties and the second in the fifties. The officials of Lakeside Co. thought that probably the 18–25-year-old group were mainly narcotics addicts and the 50–60-year-old men were likely alcoholic vagrants.

A very different picture is given when the distribution of the shoplifters who were apprehended with merchandise valued at less than $5.00 is plotted according to age and sex (Chart 2). The findings also indicate a substantial difference between the behavior of people in middle life as contrasted with the behavior of the young and the old. This will be discussed further after we have considered the kinds of merchandise stolen.

Among women who stole merchandise valued at under $5.00, a considerable difference occurred between the age group "under 15" (who more frequently stole the less expensive merchandise) and those of 15–19 years of age (C.R. 2.2). After age 19 the proportion of women who stole inexpensive merchandise remained at about 40 per cent until age 70. Of women over 70, 73 per cent stole items valued at $5.00 or less. This represented a slump of 30 per cent from the preceding age period 60–69. The finding, as we shall see, has significance when related to other data indicating the motivation of shoplifters.

The evidence thus shows that about 30 to 40 per cent of adult men, in the Store sample of shoplifters at age levels between 20 and 70, stole relatively valuable merchandise ($20.00 or more). The proportion of women who took merchandise valued at over $20.00 varied more with age, ranging from 10 per cent to 30 per cent, with a higher proportion of women in the middle years taking more valuable items. Girls were more often, age for age, involved in the theft of valuable merchandise than were boys (C.R. 3.46).

In summary, for most shoplifters in this department store, the individual crime was the theft of goods of such small value as to make it most unlikely that the sale of the goods through illegal channels was the major consideration involved. Of all persons arrested for shoplifting, about two-thirds had in their possession merchandise valued at under $20.00, and about one-half had merchandise valued at under $10.00.

KINDS OF MERCHANDISE STOLEN

The noncommercial nature of most department store shoplifting is suggested not only by the value of the merchandise stolen but by the nature of the merchandise. Commercial shoplifters take goods for which they know a ready market exists or for which they have taken "orders" in advance of the theft. They also, of course, pilfer merchandise for their own use. Detectives tell stories of arresting a person for stealing a packet of razor blades and finding that he also had several hundred dollars worth of valuable merchandise hidden on his person.

Men's and women's suits and coats, women's dresses, luggage, radios, cameras, and other similar equipment are favorite articles for commercial shoplifters. And in urban areas it is not unusual for a booster to offer to acquire articles of merchandise of a given color and size for someone. The unwary buyer may discover, however, that he has bought goods of an inferior quality with the label of a "name" store as the only genuine part of the sale. To protect their reputation, "name stores" carefully lock unattached labels into safes at night.

Television sets, office typewriters and other objects too bulky to be carried unobtrusively out of stores are also stolen by professional thieves. A relatively simple technique is "worked" for smaller appliance stores: The thief steals a sales slip and fills it out with the specifications of the article to be stolen. Marking the sales slip "paid," he forges the manager's signature. When the manager is observed to leave the store, perhaps for lunch, the thief presents the sales slip to a clerk saying that he now has his car at the loading platform ready to receive the merchandise he has "bought." The obliging clerk may help him

carry out the stolen article. Since thefts by this technique
are well guarded against in department stores, no instances
of this kind were found in the data. In any case they are,
perhaps, not strictly "shoplifting."

The various means by which professional thieves "purchase" merchandise by the use of stolen charge plates are
also outside the scope of this study. This practice is, however, very common. Sometimes it involves delivery of the
merchandise by the store to a home where someone posing
as a member of the family or a maid signs a receipt for
the delivery of the merchandise. It is, of course, quickly removed from the premises.

The merchandise most frequently recovered by store detectives from all shoplifters (men, women, and children)
was classified into 25 categories. The most frequent thefts
(involving more than 100 people each) were of jewelry,
dress accessories, billfolds and other small leather goods,
women's clothing (other than dresses, coats, and suits).
Books, purses, cosmetics, stationery, bric-a-brac, and hats
had 50–100 "takers" each. Women's suits and coats, toys,
household supplies, notions, and food were found in the
possession of 25 to 50 people.

Men's suits and coats, all umbrellas, shoes, and cloth
remnants were taken by fewer than 25 people. This inventory which is of the merchandise recovered from all
people: men, women, and children, can be compared with
the list of merchandise stolen by adult women given in
Table 1 p. 86.

The most popular goods for shoplifting are relatively
small and easily concealed and are, for this reason no
doubt, attractive to pilferers. Moreover displays of these
goods are most carefully watched. The practice of watching
these goods both reflects the store detectives' past experi-

ence that such lines of merchandise are among the most frequently taken and also contributes largely to the total number of arrests.

In the examination of the records of merchandise stolen by women who were prosecuted in the Women's Court, it was observed that one department store (not Lakeside Co.) charged a very large number of women with the theft of handbags. Inquiry disclosed that this store carried an unusually large line of handbags and kept a detective watching this display constantly.

Spectacular thefts of bulky items directly from display are rare. There are no illustrations of such thefts in the Store data, but detectives, who remember such instances vividly report that items of furniture and demonstrator vacuum sweepers have been recovered from thieves. Lawrence Klingman in an amusing article[2] about shoplifting tells of an incident in which a detective observed a man lift an aluminum kayak and balance it on his head.

He followed the man down six flights of stairs, past half a dozen store guards, out to a jammed Herald Square, and for several blocks down crowded streets to a parked car, where the man began to tie the kayak to its roof. At this point Campion flashed his badge. The shoplifter's reaction was more astonishment than dismay.

Although the kinds of merchandise stolen by adult women (shown in Table 1, p. 86) is revealing in itself, it is even more revealing when it is compared with the merchandise that is *not* stolen. In the Lakeside Co. records, dress accessories, jewelry, women's clothing, and small leather goods lead the list of things most frequently shoplifted. Children's clothing, however, does not appear on the list at all, and only one per cent of women were appre-

2. Klingman, Lawrence, *Park East*. January, 1953.

hended with stolen men's clothing in their possession. Yet the Store has, as we have noted, a large men's department and it also has an impressive selection of infants' and children's wear. A large part of the floor space in Lakeside Co. is given over to the display of useful household objects (towels, sheets, pillowcases, table wear, and the like) and a large part of the sales volume of the store comes from these sections. Fewer than six per cent of arrested women, however, had shoplifted anything that could be classified either as "equipment" or as a household object.

The examination of the individual records from which Table I was compiled shows that when merchandise not suitable for sale (merchandise of small value) was stolen it was undoubtedly for the pilferer's own personal use—not for her husband, her children, or her household. It might be added that food stores report that small tins of "fancy goods" are the most frequently stolen.)

In Chapter VII we will attempt further examination of the significance of these findings in relation to shoplifters' motivations, but the bare fact may here be recorded that the kinds of merchandise pilfered by women are not necessities or useful basic goods; they are chiefly luxury goods, and they are things which women desire for themselves but find it difficult to justify purchasing within a restricted budget.

NUMBER OF ITEMS OF MERCHANDISE STOLEN

The number of articles of stolen merchandise found in the possession of shoplifters arrested in Lakeside Co. ranged from one to 36. Forty-six per cent of the adult

men and 60 per cent of the adult women were carrying
at the time of arrest more than one stolen object. It is
possible that some of those who stole only one thing could
have been impulsive people overcome by an uncontrollable
urge to seize upon some displayed object. It is very difficult, however, to believe this of people who stole more
than once in a single day. The shoplifter who walks about
the store stealing a piece of jewelry in one place and a belt
in another has usually come into the store with the intent
to steal, and, in all probability, has had prior experience in
shoplifting.

Whereas possessing more than one piece of stolen merchandise would seem to indicate deliberate and intentional
theft, having stolen only one article does not necessarily
imply the absence of premeditated intent to steal. Professional shoplifters sometimes steal only one thing at a
time, taking it from the store and placing it in a car or a
public locker before returning to steal more. A confirmed
pilferer may have only one stolen item in his possession
because he was caught at the beginning of his day's tour
or because he intended to steal only that one thing on that
particular day.

Data on the number of items stolen throw some light on
differences in techniques of shoplifting. Men significantly
more often than women steal only one thing (54 per cent of
men to 39 per cent of women, C.R. 3.4). Also men steal
more than five things less often than women (7 per cent vs.
18 per cent C.R. 4.4). The observation of store detectives
that it is more difficult to apprehend men than women because men just take one object and then get out of the
store is thus confirmed. "People," said one detective, "steal
in the same way they buy. A man comes in with something

definite in mind. He sees it; takes it, and he leaves. Women shop around. They look at this and that, handle the merchandise, feel it, smell it, put it down, come back and go away again. It's just the way they shop. They're not sure if they want it or don't. You go crazy watching them, but if you're not sure enough to pick them up on the first thing they steal, you can follow them until they take something else."

The fact that women steal more objects than men in a single tour of the store suggests that in relation to the actual number of persons involved in department store shoplifting, men may very well be underrepresented in store arrest figures since the chance of being arrested is improved with each new theft.

The differences between boys and girls in respect to the number of articles stolen are not as great as between men and women although the direction of the difference is the same. Boys more often than girls, apparently, take only one thing (C.R. 1.0). Men and boys steal the fewest items, women the most. Among adults there would appear to be no consistent or significant relationship between age and the number of articles stolen.

These data, however, could be susceptible of another explanation, namely the practices of the store police, a fact which, as has been pointed out, can influence all arrest statistics. It is probably easier to obtain a conviction in the court of men and boys than of women and girls, and therefore it would be expedient for store detectives—who want their arrests substantiated—to establish a greater certainty of guilt for women and girls. An examination of merchandise stolen from stores other than Lakeside Co. and found in the possession of the Store's arrested shoplifters tends, however, to minimize the importance of this factor.

MERCHANDISE FROM OTHER STORES

Just as women steal more things than men in a single tour of Lakeside Co., so they more often have merchandise stolen from other stores in their possession when arrested. Women are found with merchandise stolen from other stores about five times as frequently as men. Girls also have merchandise from other stores slightly more often than boys. On the other hand, the differences between men and boys and between women and girls in this regard are not marked nor are they statistically reliable. However, just as the number of objects stolen from Lakeside Co. differs with sex, the tendency of women to steal merchandise in several stores increases their chances for arrest relative to those of men.

SUMMARY: STORE DATA

The Store data on the nature of the crime show, although not always as directly as might be wished, that "habitual" or "systematic" pilferers exist. (Or one might call them "sophisticated pilferers.") They are persons, that is to say, who make a practice of stealing rather than of buying from retail stores part of the merchandise they use. The data also show that these habitual pilferers make up a large segment of all store arrests. Commercial or occupational thieves also shoplift, some of them even "professionally." Apparently systematic pilferers and commercial thieves are the two major groups contributing to the practical problem of shoplifting. If there are people who impetuously steal only one thing in their lives, or who, when they entered the store, had no thought or intention of stealing, but yielded to a momentary impulse, they cannot form the bulk of shoplifters, nor are they financially an important group with which department store managements must deal. Department store protection officials think such impulsive individuals exist only rarely and not in sufficient numbers to make any significant part of the shoplifting problem. The point is stressed because it is so much a part of the popular folklore of shoplifting that such impetuous and impulsive individuals, on the one hand, and a small group of professional thieves, on the other, make up the shoplifting population.

Arrested persons frequently claim that their theft was a unique event, but with depressing frequency search reveals other stolen merchandise in their possession.

In summary, on any one day women steal a greater number of articles than men. Because women steal more objects, their relative chance of arrest is greater than that of men, for the store detectives must observe the shoplifter in the act of stealing before arrest can be made. This would suggest that in reality a larger proportion of department store shoplifters are men than appear in the arrest data. The mean and median values of merchandise stolen by men are larger than the values of merchandise stolen by women.

Again it should be noted here that we are dealing with a department store, and the bulk of the customers are women. What the picture would be if we had data on thefts from automotive supply shops, sporting goods stores, electrical equipment stores, bookstores, camera shops, and the like is not known.

COURT DATA

As was pointed out in Chapter III, the data of Lakeside Co. were not the only source of information used in this study. The data of two Municipal Court branches were examined and the arrest records of the Chicago Police Department were consulted. As the records of the Women's Court (Branch 40) of the Chicago Municipal Court furnished most of the useful data, the information gleaned from this source relevant to the understanding of the offense will be examined first.

Information about the thefts of women who were officially charged with shoplifting in the Chicago Municipal Court is less useful in showing the nature of the criminal behavior than are the Store data, for the Municipal Court data are only for women 18 years old and older, and they represent a selection from the store arrests made chiefly by 10 department stores. They therefore reflect only the apprehension of *some* of the shoplifters in settings in which private police are employed. Of the 873 prosecution records of women examined, 801 were initiated on the complaint of 15 department stores; 40 were from complaints brought by clothing stores; all drug stores in Chicago accounted for only 3 arrests; all variety stores (5 and 10 cent stores), 12; and grocery stores, 17; camera, record, book and appliance stores 0. The screening by stores for purposes of prosecution discussed in part in Chapter I involves a complex of factors aimed mainly at selecting the more serious offenders (although in some stores this practice may be abandoned temporarily in favor of "cracking down" on everyone guilty of theft). Court records show that 52 per cent of the 873 women in the sample were charged with

Table 1
Kinds of Merchandise Stolen by Adult Women
(Women's Court and Lakeside Co. Data)

"Kind" of Merchandise	COURT Number	Per cent*	LAKESIDE CO. Number	Per cent*
Jewelry	72	8.1	201	28.4
Billfolds	9	1.0	88	11.1
Toys	6	.7	11	1.6
Bric-a-Brac	8	.9	45	6.4
Books, records	6	.7	48	6.8
Stationery	3	.2	43	6.1
Shoes	17	1.9	10	1.4
Umbrellas	9	1.0	13	1.8
Food	21	2.4	21	2.9
Gadgets	19	2.1	46	6.4
Equipment	11	1.2	6	.8
Household	38	4.3	33	4.7
Remnants	8	.9	11	1.5
Notions	8	.9	30	4.5
Cosmetics	36	4.0	41	5.8
W. coats and suits	106	11.8	35	4.9
W. dresses	235	26.4	62	8.8
W. clothing (other)	217	24.4	96	13.5
Dress Accessories	156	17.5	206	29.1
Purses	153	17.2	75	5.1
M. suits	10	1.1	2	.3
M. clothing (other)	21	2.4	7	1.0
Hats	26	2.9	41	5.8
Other	38	4.3	52	7.3
Not ascertained	14	1.6	11	1.5
Total Women	873		709	

* Refers to per cent of all women stealing these items. Since one woman often steals more than one item, the totals do not add to 100 per cent.

stealing merchandise of $14.95 value. Fourteen ninety-five is an "official" charge, and, at the time, the top limit for petty larceny, which had to be under $15.00. It implies the theft of goods worth that much or more, and it is obviously not an accurate evaluation of the worth of stolen merchandise. Forty-eight per cent of women were charged with stealing merchandise valued at less than $14.95, including

15 per cent of women who were charged with the theft of merchandise valued at less than $5.00 (40 per cent of Lakeside Co. adult women were actually apprehended with stolen merchandise of less than $5.00 value). Forty-five per cent of women in the Women's Court sample were charged with the theft of a single article (39 per cent of women in the store sample). These "Court" figures of the number of articles stolen, however, cannot be taken at face value. For store detectives to obtain a finding of guilty, the theft of only one thing needs to be proved. A shoplifter caught with 20 stolen articles in his possession needs to be charged only with the theft of one. And this is done on occasions in which store management is concerned chiefly with having enough witnesses to be sure of getting a finding of "guilty" rather than making a case for a jail sentence for the offender.

The Women's Court records giving the kinds of merchandise women are charged with shoplifting show a general tendency on the part of store officials to prosecute women who have stolen suits, coats, dresses, and purses (i.e., the most salable items).

CHAPTER V

WHO TOOK IT?

THE DATA of Chapter IV showed that most shoplifters are pilferers, and that most pilferers are sophisticated rather than impulsive pilferers. In this and the following chapter the data on the personal and social characteristics of the shoplifters who make up both the Store and court samples will be presented. The total data (including some 40 tables, 12 charts, and 12 maps) of which only some of the results are summarized here are available, to any interested specialist, in the original doctoral dissertation from which this book has been adapted.[1]

In overall terms, the basic distribution by age, race, and sex of the Lakeside Co. arrested shoplifters has already been discussed. About 60 per cent of all persons arrested for shoplifting in the Store were adult women, and of adults, 83 per cent were women. Boys and girls (defined as under 18) were arrested with about equal frequency. White people were arrested about 9 times as frequently as

1. Cameron, Mary B. *Department Store Shoplifting.* University Microfilms, Ann Arbor, Michigan. Publication No. 6434.

Negro people (about their proportion in the Chicago population). Chart 3, p. 90, shows the Lakeside Co. arrests as a population pyramid.

However desirable it would be to know the actual sex ratio of the shoplifters at large in Chicago or their distribution by age, race, social class, or other socio-personal characteristics, the material in this study is not, to emphasize again a point made previously, designed to give an accurate answer to this very difficult question. It is unlikely that the distribution by age, sex, race, etc., of Lakeside Co. arrests would be typical of the distribution of all shoplifters including grocery, drug, hardware, tobacco, liquor, appliance, and variety stores. One cannot even know, certainly, the degree to which Lakeside Co.'s distribution of shoplifters occurs in other department stores since the necessary statistical breakdowns are not kept by most stores. Nor can one make even a simple comparison between shoppers in general and shoplifters within one department store.

To those not familiar with department store operation, it would seem possible to check by a sampling procedure the numbers of male, female, adult and juvenile, Negro and white shoppers in the store and use these figures as a basis for a comparison with arrested shoplifters. In some small stores or speciality shops, this procedure might be possible. The enormous plant and the physical design of Lakeside Co. precluded this form of check. The numerous doors in the Store, for example, enabled people to use its aisles as short cuts to the Chicago "el" lines and to other streets. Casual observation made it apparent that the proportions of old and young, women and men varied with the store entrance at which the observation was made,

Chart 3
Number of persons stealing merchandise of different values; by age and sex

(Lakeside Co. Data)

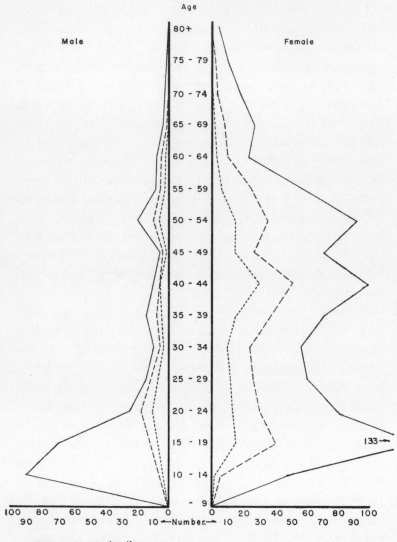

Male — Female

All merchandise

------ $ 10.00 and over value

------- $ 20.00 and over value

the day of the week, the time of day, and, especially, the weather.

It would also be interesting to compare and contrast the age, sex, race, and social backgrounds of Lakeside Co.'s pilferers with the commercial shoplifters arrested in the store. However, accurate comparison is not possible here either. Store records give no clear and certain indication into which category an individual shoplifter belongs. None of the factors which might serve as indices of commercial shoplifting (value of merchandise, etc.) is related exclusively enough to commercial shoplifting to permit it to serve as a reliable index.

In spite of all these difficulties, however, sufficient data are available to enable one to make some limited but significant generalizations. Although it does not include all that we would like it to include, the information is, nevertheless, revealing. The store data, for instance, include information on occupations of shoplifters, race, residence, age, prior criminal record and, for some shoplifters, psychiatric findings. Other similar data are available from court and police records. And although we cannot compare these data with those on the nonshoplifting shoppers we can compare them with census and other data on the general population of Chicago, and the nature of the general population can be assumed to give us at least a very rough approximation of the shopping population.

OCCUPATIONS

The Lakeside Co. records of apprehended shoplifters included information on the occupations of employed shoplifters, and for married women who were not em-

ployed, the occupations of their husbands. Although the
recorded data were not complete enough to permit any
detailed inferences, they were sufficient to show certain
patterns. In order to compare Lakeside Co's shoplifters
with the general population of Chicago, the data were
classified in the manner of the United States census.

Table 2
Employment of Arrested Shoplifters in Relation
to United States Census Employment Data, 1950

(Lakeside Co. Data)

MALE	A CHICAGO CENSUS Per cent	B MEN SHOPLIFTERS Number	Per cent	C EMPLOYED MEN SHOPLIFTERS Number	Per cent	D HUSBANDS OF WOMEN SHOPLIFTERS Number	Per cent
Professional and Managerial	19.5	6	4	6	7	35	12
Clerical	11.0	9	6	9	12	44	15
Sales	7.3	3	2	3	4	43	15
Craftsmen, Foremen	21.5	21	14	21	28	115	39
Operators, Service, and Laborers	40.4	37	25	37	49	59	20
Unemployed and others	2.0	71	48				
Total		147	99	76	100	296	101

FEMALE	E CHICAGO CENSUS Per cent	F EMPLOYED WOMEN SHOPLIFTERS Number	Per cent
Professional and Managerial	13.5	23	10.1
Clerical	37.8	25	11.0
Sales	7.1	19	8.4
Domestic and Personal service	14.3	58	25.5
Operators, Service, and Laborers	27.2	102	45.
Total		227	100

In Table 2, column A shows the 1950 census breakdown
of male occupations for Chicago in terms of percentages.
Column B is the equivalent breakdown for male shoplifters
arrested by Lakeside Co.

Forty-one per cent of arrested men were, or claimed to
be, unemployed. This figure is, at the least, extremely

Table 3
Employment Data on Arrested Shoplifters in Relation to United States Census Employment Data (1950)

(Lakeside Co. Data)

MALE	WHITE COLLAR WORKERS		MANUAL WORKERS	
	Number	Per cent	Number	Per cent
A. Chicago Population	409,000	37.8	668,000	62.0
B. Lakeside Co. Shoplifters (Unemployed considered as manual)	18	12.2	129	87.8
C. Lakeside Co. Employed Shoplifters	18	23.6	58	76.4
D. Husbands of Female Shoplifters	122	41.2	174	58.8

Difference A and B: 25.6 per cent; C.R. 9.5
Difference A and C: 14.2 per cent; C.R. 2.3
Difference A and D: 3.4 per cent; C.R. 1.19

FEMALE	WHITE COLLAR WORKERS		MANUAL WORKERS	
	Number	Per cent	Number	Per cent
E. Chicago Population	306,000	58.4	217,000	41.5
F. Lakeside Co. Employed Women Shoplifters	67	29.5	160	70.5

Difference E and F: 28.9 per cent; C.R. 9.6

doubtful. Some of these men were "unemployed," no
doubt, in the sense that their normal occupation was criminal or quasi-criminal, but it would exaggerate the numerical
importance of this group to assume that all of the people

who said they were unemployed were vocational criminals. Some of the people who stated that they were unemployed may actually have been unemployed and others may have been legitimately employed. There were pressures on arrested shoplifters both to deny employment when it existed and to claim nonexistent employment. Store detectives report that arrested men frequently exhibit great anxiety lest their employers be informed of their arrest. Since a claim of employment or unemployment made by an arrested person is not necessarily checked unless he is formally charged and brought into court, he is tempted to claim unemployment as a way of avoiding problems. On the other hand, shoplifters were under considerable pressure by the store detectives to show that they were employed since regular employment weighed heavily with the store detectives in their decision to allow the shoplifter to be released without prosecution. We must also note, however, that once a shoplifter did admit under interrogation that he was employed, or, in the case of a woman, that her husband was employed, the probability is that the facts of the employment were then stated correctly for, so far as the shoplifter knew, these facts were about to be verified.

Column D of Table 2, p. 92, shows the employment breakdown of the husbands of women shoplifters. It is presented as a very rough index of the social status of women shoplifters arrested in Lakeside Co. Column E shows the employment breakdown for women, 1950 census, and column F the employment data on employed women shoplifters. The same figures are presented in Table 3, p. 93, grouped in terms of white collar vs. manual workers. In this Table professional and managerial, clerical, and sales workers are considered white collar workers;

craftsmen, operators, service workers, and laborers are considered manual workers.

If the statements of occupation made by arrested shoplifters are even relatively correct, these data show that there is a significantly higher proportion of manual workers among the employed shoplifters, both female and male, arrested in Lakeside Co. than in the Chicago population (C.R. column C, 2.95; and column F, 9.6). Relating the "class" nature of the Store to the group arrested in it, one can say with some conviction that shoplifting is not, as a popular concept would have it, primarily an avocation of the rich and pampered.

The data on the employment status of husbands of women shoplifters show that they are about as likely to be white collar or manual workers as the average man in Chicago. But since these men are *husbands*, they have been selected already by age and other factors which would be likely to increase the proportion of white collar workers among them. The occupational comparison of husbands of women shoplifters and the total Chicago male population thus shows that women shoplifters come from families that represent a cross-section of the community (column D) and neither from among the well-to-do nor the impoverished.

The occupational distribution of Lakeside Co. shoplifters in showing a higher proportion of manual workers than in the city population as a whole, bears out the earlier statement that the "class" nature of the Store would not necessarily have a determining effect on the social class distribution of the shoplifters. Considering both the particular store and the occupational distribution of the shoplifters arrested in it, it is probable that examination of all department store records would show that very few shoplifters are persons from upper income levels, for in Chicago Lakeside Co. would attract them if, indeed, they existed. Most shoplifters would probably be middle- and lower-income people. Residential data similarly indicate this.

RACE

Negro people shopped in Lakeside Co. in considerable numbers only after 1945. Before that time neither the economics of employment opportunities for Negroes nor the Store's practices encouraged Negro trade. In the 6-year period 1945–1950, 88/867 or 10.2 per cent of all persons arrested for shoplifting were Negro. During this same period about 14 per cent (in 1940, 12 per cent; and in 1950, 15 per cent) of the population of the city was Negro. Negro people thus contributed less than their proportion in the city population to the total arrests by the Store in this period of time.

The sex distribution of Negro shoplifters in the Store was much different from that of white shoplifters. Negro men and boys constituted 57 per cent of all Negro arrests; white men and boys constituted 24 per cent of white arrests. Forty-six per cent of Negro adults arrested were men, as contrasted with 15 per cent of white adults. Compared with white women arrested in this Store, Negro women were substantially underrepresented in the arrest figures.

RESIDENTIAL DISTRIBUTION

A spot-map distribution of the residences of Lakeside Co. adult shoplifters by census area (within the Chicago city limits) was made, and the *rate* of arrest per 1,000 adult population is shown in Map 1, p. 98. The usual concentration of crime in the slum area at the center of the city as shown in studies of other crimes is *not* present. The highest rates of Store arrest extend along the shore of Lake Michigan from the far South to the far North sides. Three separate maps were also constructed; the first showed the residences of those shoplifters who had more than one stolen item of merchandise, the second, those who had only one. A third map was of the residences of juvenile shoplifters. All maps showed similar distributions, namely the distribution along Lake Michigan's shore (and, inevitably, in scattered areas with low population bases).

Effort was made to see to what extent Store shoplifters lived in the same residential areas as Store customers. Of the possible indices of Store customers' addresses, charge accounts, and merchandise delivery records were ruled out as being class selective. The addresses of persons who claimed merchandise from the "Lost and Found" department seemed to be the most adequate index available. Neither the Lakeside Co. personnel nor I could see reasons why lost and found claimants would not be a fairly representative sample of all Store customers. These lost and found claimants' addresses were obtained for the six months period, January to June, 1952. Seven hundred and fifty-six addresses were secured. They were spotted on a map, and the rate per 1000 Chicago population is indicated on Map 2, p. 99. The results show that there was a considerable differential in the rates per 1000 population of lost and found claimants for the different census areas of the city ($Q_1 = 8Q_3$). When the rates of customers, thus indicated, were compared with the rates of shoplifters, only a very slight positive relationship was found (coefficient of mean square contingency .13). The residential data were found to support the data on occupations:

Map 1. Residential addresses of all persons in sample arrested for shoplifting 1943–1950. Rate per 1,000 Chicago 1950 population. N = 626
(Lakeside Co. Data)

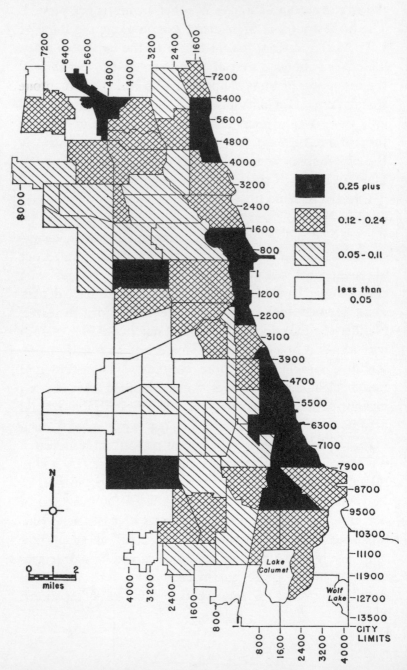

0.25 plus

0.12 - 0.24

0.05 - 0.11

less than 0.05

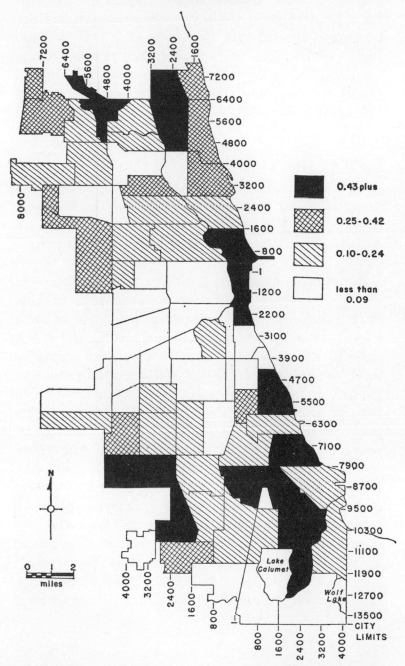

Map 2. Lost and found claimants. Rate per 1,000 Chicago 1950 population. N = 556

(Lakeside Co. Data)

0.43 plus

0.25-0.42

0.10-0.24

less than 0.09

namely, Lakeside Co. shoplifters represent a somewhat lower socio-economic and hence different residential distribution from Lakeside Co. shoppers. (They are also from very different residential areas than persons prosecuted in the Chicago Municipal Court [Branch 40, Women's Court] for shoplifting. This question will be discussed further in Chapter VI.)

PERSONS STEALING ONE ITEM ONLY

The data presented earlier showed that most shoplifters were stealing for use rather than for sale (i.e., they were pilferers) and we reasoned that a large proportion of pilferers probably had stolen merchandise with some regularity.

In this chapter, the data show that most shoplifters are also "respectable" people. Only a small proportion of shoplifters (and for women, even a small proportion of those officially charged) have prior criminal records. But is this apparent respectability of shoplifters confined largely to those who stole only one thing? We have already seen that previous data on pilferers indicate that there are not two types of pilferers as might be supposed: a first type composed of respectable people without prior criminal experience who impulsively take one thing, and a second composed of borderline delinquent types who pilfer considerable amounts of merchandise from stores. The data on residential distribution also fail to show any difference between those who take only one thing and those who have more than one piece of stolen merchandise. One cannot say with the data at hand that impulsive "weak-willed" types, so to speak, do not exist; but if they do exist, economically and residentially at least, they are not different from the known habitual pilferers. The data in support of this generalization can be summarized as follows:

1. The distribution of employment categories for women who stole only one item of merchandise from Lakeside Co. was compared with those who stole more than one item. The proportions in all employment categories were similar for both groups.

2. Spot maps of addresses (and rate maps for census areas) based on Store arrests showed no different areas of residential concentration for those who stole only one item of merchandise from those who stole more than one.

3. A higher proportion of "Court" than of "Store" adult women stole only one piece of merchandise (45 per cent as against 39 per cent). A higher proportion of men than of women in the Store sample likewise stole only one thing. Both Court cases (and Branch 40, as noted, dealt only with women) and male shoplifters represent less "respectable" groups, on the whole, than do women shoplifters arrested in the Store. But as already stated this generalization from Court records cannot be taken too seriously, because to secure a conviction in court, a store needs to prove the theft of only one thing.

It follows, then, that the data on the economic and residential backgrounds of shoplifters are distorted little, if at all, by the inclusion of people who may not be systematic pilferers but impulsive individuals.

JUVENILE SHOPLIFTING

The composition of the Store sample cannot, let us note once again, be taken as reflecting the city-wide composition of shoplifters. For instance, on a city-wide basis and in neighborhood stores as well as downtown stores, it seems

probable that juveniles (and men as well) are apprehended for shoplifting in far larger proportion than appear in the Store data, which are, after all, from a downtown department store that has goods, clothing, household furnishings, etc., usually purchased by adult women as the core of its sales and of its advertising appeals.

Inasmuch as juveniles certainly comprise the major proportion of all shoplifters (and even in the Store sample they are the most frequently arrested group both in gross numbers and in proportion to their numbers in the city population) material on juvenile shoplifters deserves special consideration.

The Lakeside Co. data showed that shoplifters ranged in age from 7 years upward. Boys were arrested with a decreasing rate in proportion to their numbers in the city population at each age level from 10 years on. Girls, on the other hand, were arrested in peak numbers at about age 15.

Girls, age for age, stole merchandise of greater median value than did boys. The median value of merchandise recovered from girls was $5.00 and from boys, $3.71.

The merchandise taken by boys was chiefly small leather goods and "gadgets": cigarette lighters, flashlights, cheap cameras, and the like. Girls stole jewelry, small leather goods, and dress accessories. Juveniles of either sex are not mainly professional shoplifters; they steal for their own use. In part, probably, the differences in the merchandise stolen reflects the older age level of the girls.

Juvenile pilfering, however, is not merely a less costly version of adult pilfering. It differs in at least one important respect: it is more often done in groups. The proportion of people recorded as "with others" at the time of arrest decreases with age. Adults were almost uniformly alone; juveniles with others. About the same trend is shown for women and girls as for men and boys, although the smaller number of males makes the male trend line less regular. Of those shoplifters, both adults and juveniles, who were with others, 104/108 or 96 per cent of males and 123/137 or 90 per cent of females were with one or more persons of the same sex. They were also with persons of about the same age level. No juveniles were arrested for shoplifting when accompanied by an adult. (There were three cases of arrests of groups containing both 17 and 18 year olds, but this was only technically a juvenile being arrested with an adult.) Some people like to recount narratives of mothers who train small children to pilfer goods which the mother pushes onto the floor from the counter, but the figures show that such incidents, if they occur, must be very rare. Some rather spectacular stories are part of the folklore of shoplifting.

Seen in single year age periods, the proportion of boys alone when arrested ranged from 0 per cent for those under 9 years of age to 100 per cent of those 19 years of age (18 years, as pointed out, defines a juvenile in Illinois). Girls ranged from 0 per cent alone at 10 years to 85 per cent alone at 19 years.

Group delinquency, in other words, is characteristic of the young shoplifter and the younger he is, the more likely it is that he will be in a group. That group delinquency is *not* a phenomenon uniquely associated with either this department store, nor, apparently, with department stores in general is supported by Shaw and McKay's finding that 93.1 per cent of boys engaged in stealing had been in the company with others. What proportion of these boys were

shoplifting and what proportion were involved in other
crimes is not ascertainable from the Shaw and McKay
report.[1] No similar material seems to have been collected
for girls. However the finding of group theft on the part
of adolescents should come as no surprise. It is common
observation that adolescents (both boys and girls) do
almost everything in cliques. Illegal behavior is no different
in this respect from legal behavior, and the delinquent acts
of adolescent groups (delinquent when viewed from nor-
mative and legal outlooks) may differ little in process from
many nondelinquent acts.

PRIOR CRIMINAL RECORDS OF SHOPLIFTERS

The store protection staffs of 10 large department stores
in Chicago have three different sources from which they
can obtain information about the prior criminal activity
of persons they have apprehended. First, they consult
their own files for previous arrests within their own store.
They may also call in their store detectives and other key
personnel to observe (through a peephole or one-way mirror) the arrested person in order that they may remember
him or to ascertain whether he is someone who has been
observed behaving suspiciously in the past. Is he, for
example, someone who has repeatedly returned merchandise for refund presenting the merchandise without a sales
slip and claiming it was a gift?

The second source of knowledge of prior records of
apprehension is the private registry of apprehended persons

1. Shaw, Clifford R. and Henry D. McKay. "Report on Social Factors
in Juvenile Delinquency," *National Commission on Law Observance and
Enforcement*. Vol. II, No. 13, 1937, pp. 193–199.

cooperatively kept by these 10 State Street department stores. The Lakeside Co. protection department has an available file (as do the other nine stores) of the names and descriptions of all persons arrested on any charge by all of these stores. This file is regularly consulted. The records are filed by name and aliases but not by fingerprint; hence the occasional person who carries misleading identification could give a false name and his prior record not be detected. But such deception could not influence the data in any major way since persons without complete identification are likely to be suspected of prior experience and turned over to the city police.

The third source for knowledge of shoplifters' past records of official arrest is the Chicago Police Department (Bureau of Identification) file of *all* official arrests in the city. Information in this file is available to stores, however, only for persons who are formally charged. When available, the information is copied into store records and kept for possible future use.

Because the Chicago Police Department records of misdemeanants are mainly records of local arrests, prior arrests for shoplifting or other charges outside Chicago would probably not be discovered. The number of persons with "prior records" who appear in the Store data is thus a minimum number (as are all figures on recidivism). However it is a record of prior *arrests* and not only of convictions, and it draws on both public and private sources instead of the single public source from which most estimates on the frequency of recidivism are drawn. How a rate of recidivism computed on this base compares with other rates of recidivism computed on different bases is difficult to assess, but certainly the Store data are more inclusive. For instance all persons who have previously been arrested in the Chicago "loop" for shoplifting by department store police appear in the Store records as recidivists, whereas official records give only those who have been prosecuted.

Of the 709 adult women in the Lakeside Co. data, only 20 (or less than one per cent) had records of having been previously arrested by any of the 10 department stores or appear in the records at the city police Bureau of Identification. This is, of course, an almost unbelievably low rate of rearrest. Although information on some of these 20 individuals was too scanty to enable sound judgment to be made on whether they were commercial shoplifters, there was sufficient information noted in the records to establish clearly that at least 7 of the 20 shoplifted commercially (i.e., were boosters). Thus *not more* than 2 per cent of women *pilferers* who were arrested by store detectives had been arrested before. Among all men arrested in the Store, 18/147 (12 per cent) had prior records. Of these 18, 10 were either narcotics addicts or criminals by occupation, thus leaving about 6 per cent as the *maximum* proportion of male *pilferers* with more than one arrest.

Thus the evidence of both official police records and unofficial department store files supports the view that pilferers once caught are almost never repeaters. Those who were brought into court, probation investigators frequently described as of "good social standing and reputation in the community." In any event, the bulk of pilferers (although apparently they had been stealing prior to their arrest with some frequency, regularity, and sophistication) have no prior experience with arrest and prosecution for crimes; they are not career criminals. The data available on the occupational distribution of adults arrested by Lakeside Co. support this view as does the information recorded for the Court cases.

OFFICIAL RECORDS OF ARREST OF CONVICTED SHOPLIFTERS

It was possible to obtain from the Police Bureau of Identification information about the criminal records of 112 persons who had been convicted of shoplifting. Some knowledge of the setting in which this information on misdemeanants is normally used in useful in appraising its relevance.

The Chicago Municipal Court is a misdemeanant court presided over by a judge who alone hears the testimony of the prosecution and defense. The court does not conduct jury trials. When the defendant has been found "guilty," the judge may consult with a social worker assigned to the court or send the offender for psychological examination before passing sentence. The judge may use the statements of the psychiatrist and social workers in addition to those of the prosecutor and the defense attorney in determining the sentence.

Trials in the Municipal Court are usually very brief and the court docket crowded. In a typical trial the judge hears the prosecution and the defense; asks questions of the defendant; asks the prosecutor for the defendant's prior record (which is kept by the Bureau of Identification); and inquires about information the social worker may have. If the defendant is a first offender and appears to be a pilferer (and is a woman), she will very likely be found "guilty," admonished by the judge, and sentenced. Since she has usually been held in jail at least one night prior to the trial, she will frequently be given the sentence, "one day considered served, and $1.00 considered paid"; or sometimes she is given a sentence of 30 days or even 6 months which is then suspended. She may also be required to report to a probation officer.

If the prosecution, calling store detectives as witnesses, fails to prove guilt, of course, the defendant will have established ground for a civil suit for "false arrest" and then be in a position to collect "damages" from the store.

Defendants who have prior records of arrest and conviction, and who have taken merchandise of considerable value are, when found guilty, usually sentenced to jail for periods ranging from 30 days to 6 months.

The sentence received by a woman shoplifter is thus, in most cases, a good indication of the prior criminal record she has acquired. The outcome of trial for men is not equally indicative of prior record. (Men, as the Store records show, are apt to have shoplifted merchandise of greater value and thus thought to be commercial shoplifters.)

Having obtained permission to examine the prior arrest records of 112 shoplifters as they appeared in the police files, it was important to make the maximum use of this limited sample. Starting with the persons who had been convicted in downtown branches of the Municipal Court for shoplifting, the sample was selected to include the names of both men and women. Women's names were selected (including both Negro and white women) who had been given token sentences or probation (implying, it was believed, no prior arrest record) and women who had been sentenced to jail (implying prior record).

Because somewhat different procedures were used to

analyze the data for men than for women, we shall consider the two separately.

Women. The women whose criminal records were examined included 37 white women and 41 Negro women
who were matched as nearly as is possible for age. The
sample was selected to include a substantial number of
women who had received jail sentences—although the
Women's Court data as a whole showed that only 13 per
cent of all women shoplifters were given jail sentences.
This selection was made because it was useful to know not
only the proportion of women with prior records but something of the range of offenses for which these women had
previously been convicted. For this reason about half of
the cases selected for examination of prior records were
from the 13 per cent of women given jail sentences. Such
a selection, it turned out, also meant that a disproportionate number of women over the age of 25 was included.

Selected Sample for the Study of Prior Records (Women)

Race	Token Sentence or Probation	Jail Sentence	Total
White	20	17	37
Negro	18	23	41
Total	38	40	78

Both Negro and white women were selected to discover
the possibility of a racial bias in the court action; but no
reliable differences were apparent in the outcomes of the
trials. Since there was a disproportionate number of older
women in the sample, the data probably reflect the same
findings as in the charges by department stores discussed
previously; namely that excessive apprehension for shoplifting apparently is not found for Negro women as such
but only for *young* Negro women. If, therefore, a racial

bias were present in Court practices, one would expect to find it operating against young Negro women (i.e., those 25 years old and younger). With the data available it was impossible to pursue this question.

Sentences and Records of Prior Conviction
(Women)

Record	Token Sentence or Probation	Jail Sentence	Total
No prior conviction	35	24	59
Prior conviction(s)	3	16	19
Total	38	40	78

Thus the data show that 35/38 or 92 per cent of the women whose records were studied and who received token sentences, suspended sentences, or probation had not previously been convicted of any crime in Chicago, and 24/40 or 60 per cent of those who were sentenced to jail likewise had not been so convicted. The statistics generally supported the observations of judges and social workers that women whose prior records were known were usually sentenced to jail. However some women without prior records were also given jail sentences.

In the unselected records of the Women's Court which were examined (Court cases) there were 638 women who received token sentences or probation. In addition 97 women were sentenced to jail. Since the existence of prior criminal record is so very important in determining the sentence imposed once the defendant has been found guilty, the proportion of jail sentences in the small Police Department sample of 78 cases, where prior record was known, can with some justification be applied to the total sample of 735 cases. If this extrapolation from the small sample is made, then 92 per cent of the 638 women who received token sentences and 60 per cent of the 97 women who were sentenced to jail probably had not been previously convicted for any crime or misdemeanor in the city of Chicago. This would imply that 645/735 or about 90 per cent of all women tried for shoplifting were in court as "first offenders." By a similar process of reasoning, about 711 of 833 or 85 per cent of women had not previously been officially *arrested* for any crime at all in the city. There was also a small number of women who were fined, who were found "not guilty," or whose sentences were vacated. These were not considered in the above rough estimates.

Among the 21 women for whom there were records of prior arrests (two of them had been arrested previously but not convicted) the number of prior arrests was as follows:

Number of Arrests	Number of Women
1	6
2–3	5
4–10	4
11 or more	6

The range in the number of arrests was from one to 22. The kinds of criminal behavior for which these 21 women had been arrested prior to the particular shoplifting arrest which brought them into the sample fall into three fairly distinct patterns: shoplifting, prostitution, and narcotics addiction. Eight had been arrested on vice charges only, and an additional eight had been arrested on both vice charges and narcotics addiction. In addition to these 21 who had prior arrest records, nine more women had been arrested subsequent to their arrest for shoplifting. The total of 30 cases, including subsequent and prior records show that 75 per cent of the women shoplifters in this selected sample who had criminal records were known to have been involved in sex offenses, and 47 per cent were known narcotics addicts.

Of the five women who had one or more prior arrests for shoplifting but had otherwise not been arrested, the names of three were recognized by one store detective as well-known shoplifters ("heels") who regularly stole valuable merchandise for illegal sale to "customers." The other two could also have been "heels" or they could have been repeating pilferers (or compulsive, neurotic thieves). There was no way to ascertain. They had not, however, been referred by the Court for psychiatric examination. If the need for this procedure had been suspected by the Court or if the defendant's attorney had requested it, an examination would have been ordered. There were, thus, at most, two possible "kleptomaniacs" in the data. Had there been "kleptomaniacs" they would have been revealed by the research procedures.

Arrest for other crimes aside from prostitution, narcotics addiction, and shoplifting was found in the records of 10 of the 30 women. These included gambling (policy), 5 women; burglary, one woman; fighting, one woman; possessing a counterfeit $10.00 bill, one woman.

The following conclusions are suggested by these data and by the extrapolation of the probable proportions of the purposeful sample (78 cases) to the total Court sample (873 cases):

1. About 85 per cent of women brought into court on shoplifting charges probably had no prior local arrests, and 90 per cent had apparently never been convicted of any crime.

2. The sample of 30 women with prior or subsequent arrest records showed mainly arrests for prostitution and narcotics addiction or both. A small number of women

(five) were repeatedly arrested for shoplifting but for no other offense. Three of these were well-known professionals. The other two may have been also.

Men: In addition to the records for women, the records of the prosecutions for petty larceny of the first 100 men tried in 1952 in the downtown branch of the Chicago Municipal Court were examined. Of these 100, 44 had been arrested for shoplifting and 56 for other forms of larceny. The disposition of the cases of the 44 men shoplifters was as follows:

Record	Number of Men
Not found guilty (including: not guilty, nolle pros., discharged without prosecution)	2
Token sentence or probation	5
30 days jail sentence (or less)	14
60 days jail sentence (or more)	20
Not ascertainable	3
Total	44

The prior and subsequent police records of arrest and conviction of the 34 men sentenced to jail were examined. The records of the seven who were not found guilty, given token sentences, or given probation were not examined. It was assumed because of the sentence that this group had no prior criminal record.

Of the 34 men shoplifters who were sentenced to jail, 12 had no prior convictions in Chicago and 22 had been convicted one or more times. Of these, two had nine convictions each.

The kinds of crimes previously and subsequently charged against men who were convicted of shoplifting and sentenced to jail ranged from begging to murder. Narcotics addiction apparently played a part in the lives of 16 per cent of the men, and chronic alcoholism (as revealed in repeated arrests for drunkenness) in 18 per cent. Other than these two patterns of behavior, 11 per cent had been convicted for operating gaming establishments. Other criminal records included assault and battery, indecent exposure, rape, begging, fighting, accessory after the fact, assault with intent to kill, resisting arrest, running a confidence game, receiving stolen property, peddling narcotics, jackrolling, till tapping. Fifteen of the total of 44 (34 per cent) had previously been arrested for shoplifting.

If it can be assumed that those receiving token sentences and probation and those not found guilty had not previously been convicted of crimes, then 19/41 or 46 per cent of men in this small sample of those officially arrested for shoplifting had no prior criminal convictions.[2] This compares with about 90 per cent of women.

In addition to the 22 men with prior convictions, five men had previously been arrested but not convicted. Thus a total of at least 27/41 or 66 per cent of all men shoplifters in this sample had previously been arrested in Chicago. Not more than 14/41 or 34 per cent had never been arrested in the city. (This includes seven whose police records were examined and no prior arrests found; and seven whose police records were not examined [but who were not sentenced to jail]. Five of these latter received token sentences or probation and it is thus assumed there were no prior arrests; two were not found guilty and were likewise

2. In 1952, 62 per cent of all men and 46 per cent of women whose fingerprints were sent to the FBI had prior fingerprint arrest records as revealed by the FBI. (*Uniform Crime Reports*, XXII, 2, 1951), but direct comparison is not possible between the FBI records and the police records that formed the base for this section of the study on shoplifters. The records checked here were more complete for the local area than the FBI records (the fingerprints of most misdemeanants are not sent to the FBI), but they are confined to the Chicago area.

assumed not to have been previously arrested.) The 34
per cent of men contrasts with 85 per cent of women who
had no prior record of arrests. The over-all picture of the
prior arrest records of women shoplifters shows, in summary (and by the extrapolation of the proportions in a
selected sample to the total sample for women), that a
large proportion of women were without prior local criminal records. Many more men shoplifters had local criminal
records. In the sample studied here 66 per cent of men and
10 to 15 per cent of women were estimated to have prior
arrest records. Since these people had been screened already by department store staffs, those who were formally
charged with shoplifting certainly had a higher proportion
of persons who had prior arrest records than shoplifters as
a whole.

In combination with the Store data which showed that
men took merchandise of greater median and mean value
than women, the data on prior arrest records suggests that
men shoplifters are more often "boosters" than women.

PSYCHIATRIC FINDINGS

One further item of information was available which,
in a negative way at least, shows something of the personal
characteristics of the 873 women who were officially
charged with shoplifting in the Municipal Court ("Court
sample"). Of these women 56 (6.5 per cent) were referred
by the court for examination by the court psychiatric
service. Twelve (1.4 per cent) of the 873 women were
found to be committable to the Chicago Psychopathic
Hospital for further examination before disposition of

their cases. Since this is the procedure regularly followed with suspected psychotics, there thus seems to be a relatively insignificant relationship between shoplifting and actual or probable *psychosis*. Nor does there seem to be, as we shall see, a close relationship between shoplifting and recognizably neurotic behavior.

Of the remaining 44 women who were referred for psychiatric examination, two were not examined, two were reported as having no specific psychiatric disability, two were diagnosed as showing evidence of central nervous system pathology, one was found to be a simple mental deficient. Four others were narcotics addicts who had reached the Municipal Court on a larceny charge instead of being "booked" on a narcotics charge. The range of the psychiatric diagnoses of the remaining 33 is shown below:

Psychiatric Diagnoses	Number of women
Involutional reaction	8
Reactive depression	4
Emotional instability	2
Emotional immaturity	6
Compulsive neurosis	4
Adult maladjustment	2
Psychoneurosis with alcoholism	2
Schizoid personality	1
Hysterical with fugue states	1
Paranoid trend	1
Inadequate personality	1
Kleptomania with simple adult maladjustment	1
Total	33

On the basis of these findings, it appears that psychiatric diagnosis did not reveal any characteristic trends of neurotic personality deviation among those shoplifters who were

examined. It is also evident that some of these diagnoses
(perhaps, most of them) imply no more than that the
woman caught shoplifting was upset about being arrested.

At this point it seems worthwhile to discuss a term I
have not found necessary or useful to employ often in this
study, "kleptomania." The term was common in nine-
teenth-century psychology. It was one of the monomanias
in the elaborate classificatory system developed by Pinel,
followed by Esquirol and Griesinger. Only a few terms of
their taxonomy of manias and phobias have survived in
modern descriptive terminology, e.g., nymphomania, dipso-
mania, pyromania, and kleptomania. Their systems of
psychology have been generally rejected by modern thera-
pists. There neither are (nor in terms of modern psychology, ever were) "kleptomaniacs," i.e., people whose
only form of maladjustment is an obsessive-compulsive
desire to steal. But there probably are disturbed people,
neurotic and psychotic people, for whom *one* symptom of
their disturbance is the stealing of merchandise from stores.

No modern psychotherapist, however, would assume
that "kleptomania" is an entity which can be treated apart
from the total personality configuration of the individual.
At a later point in this study the question of the psychiatric implication of the data on shoplifters will be discussed
in the context of its contribution to theories of crime
causation.

SUMMARY

I. The evidence presented in the previous chapter
showed that most shoplifting is pilfering rather than commercial theft. The evidence presented in this chapter shows

that most shoplifters, especially most women shoplifters, are "respectable" people. For the most part they are people who lack the kinds of prior criminal experience which would indicate extensive association with a criminal subculture. They accept the dominant social values with regard to law-abiding behavior even though they deviate from them.

A. Of Store arrests, 12 per cent of men and three per cent of women were known to have been arrested previously either by department stores or by the city police. Extrapolation from the proportions of a small sample to the total "Court sample" of women suggests that only about 10 per cent to 15 per cent of women prosecuted in the Chicago Municipal Court for shoplifting had previously been arrested by the Chicago police. Sixty-six per cent of a small sample of men charged with shoplifting had prior arrests in Chicago.

B. The residential distribution of Lakeside Co. arrests for shoplifting showed no concentration either of juveniles or adults in the slum and "ghetto" areas of Chicago; nor was there a concentration in "gold coast" areas.

C. The occupational distribution of Lakeside Co. arrested shoplifters differs with sex.

1. *Women:* The *husbands* of nonworking, married, women shoplifters are reported as being white collar workers in approximately the same proportion as all *males* (including those too young to be white collar workers) in the city population. Employed women shoplifters are probably more frequently manual workers than employed women in the city population. Taking into consideration both the occupational distribution of women shoplifters in the Store and the "class" nature of the store, it seems reasonable to

conclude that well-to-do women shoplift in department stores considerably less frequently than middle- and lower-class women. The reasoning involved here is that if wealthy women shoplifted in Chicago with relatively as great frequency as middle- and lower-income women, they would be grossly over-represented in the arrests of Lakeside Co. (since it is one of very few stores in which they would do their shoplifting). This is not so, and in fact, they are under-represented. It would appear that the actual rate of shoplifting by well-to-do women must be quite low. On the basis of both statistical and observed facts and impressions, the folklore stereotype of the woman shoplifter as a neurotic upper-middle-class woman is not confirmed. Neither is the female pilferer a recognizable member of a criminal or deliquent subculture.

And at this point it is probably well to bring in our hypothetical "little old lady" who is allowed to shoplift with impunity and the goods charged to her son's account. She is reported from coast to coast. Her son is usually a prominent politician or physician or someone equally in the public eye. ("She" is never a "little old man.") Conceivably she might exist in a very small community with only one or two "general stores." She could not exist in a modern urban area. No merchant could legally become an "accessory to the fact" by allowing this procedure, and no one so disturbed as the "little old lady" could be safely allowed to roam the streets and stores unaccompanied. If, in fact, such disturbed elderly people were picked up by store detectives, and occasionally they are, the detectives would certainly contact their children and suggest that the elderly person no longer be allowed in the store unless accompanied by a responsible adult.

2. *Men:* The Store evidence on the occupational distribution of men shoplifters is, for reasons discussed, probably not wholly reliable, but it still appears likely that a somewhat smaller proportion of men shoplifters are upper- or middle-class people than would be expected in a random cross section of the city population.

D. Of the Store shoplifters who have previous arrest records, there is sufficient evidence to show that most are commercial shoplifters stealing for sale rather than for personal use of the merchandise. Not more than two per cent of women and six per cent of men arrested in the Store could possibly have been repeating (re-arrested) pilferers, and evidence on these persons was insufficient to show whether all of them were pilferers or some or all were commercial shoplifters.

II. The low rate of recidivism found for pilferers in both Store and Court data is evidence not only of the "respectability" of pilferers, but it is also evidence against regarding shoplifting as a form of compulsion-neurosis or kleptomania. Additional evidence is found in the fact that only five of 57 women examined by court psychiatrists were so diagnosed. There is thus *nothing at all* in the data to support the widespread popular belief that shoplifters (especially women shoplifters) are compulsive neurotic personalities irrationally stealing merchandise. This point will be discussed at length in a following chapter.

CHAPTER VI

MIDDLE-CLASS CRIME

AND PUBLIC STATISTICS

AS WAS NOTED in the introductory chapters, the total material presented in this study has two central aspects: first, the study of shoplifting as a crime and the socio-personal characteristics of the people arrested committing this crime; second, the selective processes of a private police agency determining which arrested persons will be charged with crime and which allowed to go free without being turned over to the public police. Data on shoplifting and shoplifters have been presented in Chapters IV and V. In this chapter, the chief emphasis will be on the functioning of the department store protection service as an agency prejudging arrested persons by selecting from the total arrests those who will be prosecuted and those who will not. These matters obviously have further bearing on those previously discussed: the extent of shoplifting and the age, sex, race, and social class distribution of apprehended shoplifters.

121

EXTENT OF SHOPLIFTING

Exact information on the extent of shoplifting is impossible to obtain. It is difficult even to obtain sociologically useful information on the number of *department store* arrests for shoplifting. The reluctance of department store officials to discuss this problem can be overcome, but stores do not keep the necessary breakdowns of their data classified according to offense and offender. What total arrest records they do keep—as we have noted—include stockroom and warehouse thieves, drunks, sex offenders, purse snatchers, pickpockets, and employee thefts as well as shoplifting arrests. Moreover, even among shoplifters, juveniles constitute a considerable section of arrests, and juveniles are not necessarily recorded separately in store summaries as they are in court records. It is thus impossible to estimate on a city-wide basis the number of arrests or even of department store arrests for shoplifting that do *not* come to official attention and compare the estimate with official arrest figures.

Only one previous study on the subject seems to exist, a monograph by Sellin who compared thefts in three Philadelphia department stores[1] (1928–33) with thefts known to the police of that city. His conclusion was that almost as many thefts were known but unreported by the three department stores as were known to the police of the entire city. He did not say, however, how he arrived at the number of *thefts* known to department stores, and he is probably inaccurate in believing, as he apparently did, that all these are shoplifting thefts. (Unless he estimated an average of about four stolen items per shoplifter.)

1. Sellin, Thorsten. *Research Memorandum on Crime in the Depression.* Social Science Research Council, Bulletin 27, 1937.

His data run as follows: in 1928, 4,935 thefts were known to the three stores; arrests by detectives were 1,147; and 227 persons were prosecuted and convicted; 6,318 thefts were known to the police of the entire city. In 1933 the figures were 5,314 thefts known to the three stores; 1,432 arrests were made by store detectives; 230 people were prosecuted and convicted; 7,402 thefts were known to the police.

Since, as said before, specific acts of shoplifting cannot be known to have taken place aside from apprehending the offender, the form of comparison used by Sellin cannot give exactly relevant figures. In round numbers, however, Lakeside Co. data for adult women shoplifters can be compared with official arrest figures for larceny by women since all women were tried in the same branch of the court Between 1943 and 1949 the Chicago Police Department[2] reported an average of 633 women charged with larceny per year. Between 1943 and 1949, Lakeside Co. arrested for shoplifting an average of 405 women per year of whom only 10 per cent or 40 per year were officially charged. One department store, in other words, *arrested* for shoplifting about 60 per cent of the total number of women per year as were officially charged with all types of larceny (including shoplifting) in the entire city of Chicago.

The proportion found for women, however, does not apply to men. In the same time period an average of 2,479 men per year were charged with larceny by the Chicago Police Department. In the Store between 1943 and 1949 an average of 84 men were arrested per year for shoplifting and 35 per cent or 29 men were prosecuted. Instead of a

2. Chicago Police Department, *Annual Reports*. This figure includes grand as well as petty larceny.

ratio of 2:3 between Store arrests and all police charges of larceny in the city as found for women, the ratio is 84/2,479 or 1:30 for men.

The differences in the ratios of Stores and public arrest between women and men is of course the result of the fact that men are much more frequently involved in occupations which include larceny than women. Men are more apt to be apprehended directly by the public police when engaged in larceny other than department store shoplifting.

All department store police in Chicago must handle a considerably larger number of larceny cases of women than are officially arrested by the city police.

AGE OF WOMEN SHOPLIFTERS

The question of the age of women criminals has been given some special consideration in criminological literature largely because of the theory that women are particularly prone to commit crimes during periods of emotional upset. Von Hentig, for instance states:

Statistics reveal a distinct rise in the older female age groups which coincides with the climacteric crises. . . . There can be no doubt that there is a definite increase of female delinquency during the preclimacteric and climacteric phase.[3]

And Otto Pollak makes a considerable point of the rise of crime rates during the menopause: "The menopause . . . seems to bring about a distinct increase in crime. . . ."[4]

The syllogistic reasoning behind this concept is that (a) the menopause is a period of emotional maladjustment,

3. Von Hentig, Hans. *Crime: Causes and Conditions.* (New York, 1947), pp. 114–115.
4. Pollak, Otto. *Criminality of Women.* (Philadelphia, 1950), pp. 157–158.

and (b) crime is presumed by some psychiatrically oriented writers to be a by-product of emotional maladjustment, it follows (c) women should be particularly prone to commit crimes during the menopause. As Pollak puts it:

The student of female criminality cannot afford to overlook the generally known and recognized fact that these generative phases are frequently accompanied by psychological disturbances which may upset the need and satisfaction balance of the individual or weaken her internal inhibitions and thus become causative factors in female crime.[5]

Shoplifting arrests, as we have noted, constitute a considerable proportion (perhaps 80 per cent) of all official larceny arrests of women. (The other 20 per cent seem to be made up largely of charges against maids by employers; charges against roommates for stealing clothing or equipment; charges by men against women for pocket picking and theft of money and goods.) And some of the data on shoplifting we have seen also provide information on age. These data then can clearly have an important bearing on the "menopause theory" one way or the other.

The Store data are particularly relevant because as we have stated before, they are a much more accurate representation of the actual rates of crime (although not a perfect one) than are the official arrest rates. In Chart 3, (p. 90) the rate of arrest for shoplifting by age is depicted. From these data it would seem possible to speak only of a relatively high rate of arrest for young women in comparison with older women. In other words, contrary to Von Hentig, statistics on shoplifting do not show a "distinct rise in [the crimes of] the older female age groups which coincides with the climacteric crisis."

In Chart 4 (p. 126) which gives the *rate* of official ar-

5. *Ibid.*, p. 157.

Chart 4
Women charged with shoplifting 1948–1950; by age and race.
Rate per 10,000 Chicago 1950 female population
(Women's Court Data)

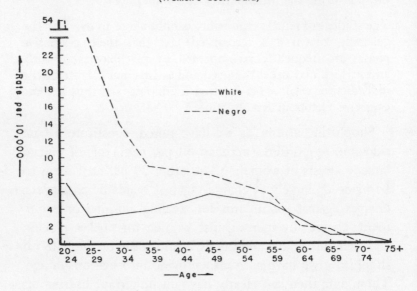

rest by age and race, it is apparent that the high rate of official arrest for young women is not at all characteristic of young women as such, but merely, statistically, of young Negro women. This finding may well be a result of the prejudiced viewpoint of store detectives who make a point of observing Negro women shoppers and who believe that young Negro women are apt to be habitual thieves. They do not have the same attitude toward older Negro women. The number of Negro women charged with shoplifting in the Court data (349) is sufficient in comparison with white women (524) to change the whole picture of arrest by age. The enormous rate of prosecution of young Negro women outbalances any other factor.

It is useful to establish the relationship of age *per se* to

Chart 5
Women charged with shoplifting 1948–1950 by age. Rate per 10,000 Chicago 1950 female population
(Women's Court Data)

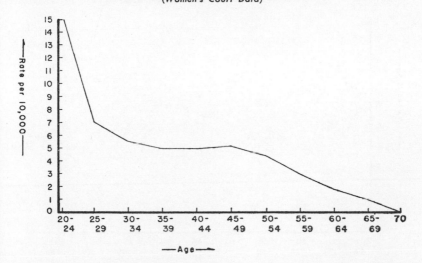

rates of larceny as this relationship appears in both Store and Court data, and since Store data have too few Negro women to make comparison by age *and* race possible, age comparisons of Store and Court data are presented for white women only. Examination of the number of official charges (Court cases) of white women in relation to the 1950 white female population of Chicago, by age, shows that the official arrest rate declined from age 20–24 to age 30–34. It picked up again at age 40–55 and declined precipitously at age 60. No women 75 years of age or over were prosecuted (Chart 5).

The Lakeside Co. arrests of white women were also examined in relation to the 1950 white female population of Chicago. To make Store and Court data comparable the rates by age were adjusted by multiplying the Court

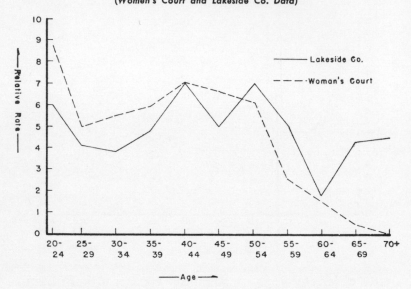

Chart 6
White women arrested for shoplifting. Rate per 10,000
Chicago white female population
(Women's Court and Lakeside Co. Data)

sample by a factor of 1.31 (there being 626 cases in the store sample and 477 in the Court sample). The comparable rates by age for the two sets of data are presented in Chart 6.

From these data there does not seem to be a high official or unofficial arrest rate for women in the climacteric years, ages 45–50. For all of the middle years, ages 25–60, the rates of both Store and Court cases are probably a fair reflection of the proportion by age not only of women shoplifters but also of women shoppers in the "loop." It seems reasonable to expect that more women in the age categories 40–60 would have the leisure to shop (and shoplift) in the "loop" stores than women 25–35, who, in greater proportion, are employed or are mothers of small children and may

well do their shopping (and shoplifting if any) in neighborhood stores. Of the 873 official charges of shoplifting that
were examined, 352 or 40 per cent were made by two
department stores (Carson, Pirie, Scott and Co. and
Mandels). These two stores and six others (Fair, Goldblatts, Marshall Field, Montgomery Ward, Sears, and
Lerner) accounted for 85 per cent of official charges of
shoplifting, and hence for 68 per cent of all official arrests
of women for petty larceny in Chicago. In neighborhood
stores shoplifters may be apprehended, as we have pointed
out, but they are not arrested and brought to official
notice.

In any event, the data show that the belief shared by
some criminologists and psychologists that crimes of
women are related to the menopause is not substantiated so
far as larceny is concerned either by Store or Court data
for white women, nor by Court data for either white or
Negro women. It is not substantiated either in gross numbers or by rate in the population. It is interesting to note
that in the Store data, the number of arrests drop from 92
at age 40–44 to 68 at age 45–49 (the most usual age for
the menopause) and the numbers and rate rise again at
age 50–54. If this variation in arrest rates indicates anything at all, the drop may signify that women suffering
from uncomfortable menopausic reactions are less likely
than other women to be in the "loop" either shopping or
shoplifting.

The comparison of rates for Store and Court cases by
age shows also a considerably higher rate of "senile delinquency" in the Store sample than had hitherto been suspected by criminologists basing their conclusions, as usual,
solely on official figures. The rate of arrest for white women
age 60–75 does not decline with age, but remains at

a level only slightly below the arrest rate for women 25–30. Older women, however, are not prosecuted in the court. Only one charge of larceny against a woman over 70 was made in Chicago in the three years covered by the Court sample. A grocery store charged a 71-year-old woman with stealing several objects. The judge in the case denied "leave to file" (an elderly woman, he said, who had hitherto led a "blameless life" should not now suffer disgrace) and the woman was not prosecuted.

AGE AND RACE

In Court cases, the rate of prosecution per 10,000 population of Negro women over the age of 35 was found to be about the same as the rate for white women of similar ages, but Negro women under 35 years of age were officially charged with larceny about six times as frequently in proportion to their number in the population as white women. There were too few adult Negro women arrested in the Store (only 21) to provide a statistically sufficient base for comparison between Store and Court data. The problem of whether the concentration of arrests of Negro women apparent in the Court data reflected actual differences in behavior or the selection procedures of various store police can only be raised but not answered. Since for store detectives an arrest must potentially be followed by a conviction, it is probable that store detectives felt freer to arrest a Negro woman with less convincing evidence than they would have considered sufficient for an arrest of a white woman.

RESIDENTIAL DISTRIBUTION OF SHOPLIFTERS

Shaw and McKay[6] and others in well known researches on the residential distribution of deliquents and criminals in Chicago found a high concentration of arrests of persons who lived in the center of the city and in the areas surrounding the center. These areas are places of physical deterioration, economic dependency, congested population, rented homes, foreign and Negro population. The interpretation given the findings has usually stressed continuing patterns of criminal behavior among the residents of the area transmitted from older to younger age groups. The persistence of the delinquent behavior is in turn thought of as a product of social disorganization in the neighborhood, of inadequate opportunities for legitimate occupations, and of personal frustration resulting from the poverty and economic exploitation of the residents.

Explanations of the so-called "delinquency areas" (the site of delinquent subcultures) have usually been based on the premise that the rate of arrest or conviction adequately or even approximately reflects the real rates of crime of those residing in different urban areas. The study of shoplifting presented an unusual opportunity to study, for this type of crime, a rate of arrest much closer to the actual crime than the official arrest rate and to compare the rate derived from the Store data with the official arrest rate. The procedure allowed some measure, even though partial and incomplete, of the degree to which the high arrest rate for ghetto areas reflects discriminations exercised against the residents. It should be kept in mind, however,

6. Shaw, Clifford R. and Henry D. McKay. *Juvenile Delinquency and Urban Areas.* (Chicago, 1942.)

that the Store arrest information, although less selected than the official arrest information, is not itself a *crime* rate. Store detectives, as was pointed out in Chapter I, are selective in their observations of people and in the arrests they make. The visible characteristics of some ghetto dwellers (race, dress, language, etc.) predispose them to store arrest just as these same characteristics act in selection for prosecution.

In order to compare the areas of concentration of Store and Court arrests, the residential addresses of arrested persons were spotted on maps according to census area. Rate maps were constructed on the basis of the 1950 census reports of the population of these areas. The Court cases show the characteristic concentration at the center of the city of the rate of arrested women per 1,000 female population (Map 3, p. 133). The rate declines as one approaches the middle and peripheral areas. (The rate is "accidently" high in certain peripheral areas where the population base is very low.) Altogether this rate-map of shoplifters resembles closely the residential maps of persons arrested for other types of crimes, or, indeed, indices of almost all other sociopathic phenomena. The rate at the first quartile of census areas is approximately 7.5 times the rate of the third quartile of census areas.

The rates by census areas of persons arrested for shoplifting at Lakeside Co., however, (Map 1, p. 98) show no such concentration at the center of the city. The dispersion is slightly greater ($Q_1 = 6 Q_3$) and the areas with the highest rates are not concentrated at the center of the city but extend along the entire shore of Lake Michigan from the 9500 block South to the 6400 block North and follow the major transportation lines. The area includes

Map 3. Residential addresses of women charged with shoplifting 1948–1950. Rate per 1,000 Chicago 1950 female population. N = 633

(Women's Court Data)

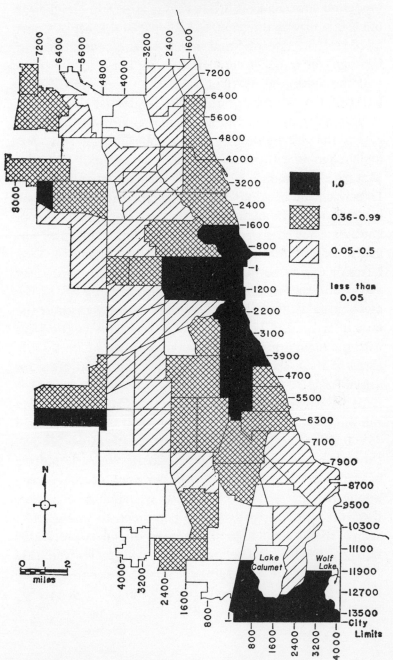

prosperous neighborhoods and communities as well as deteriorated ones. There is little or no relationship (coefficient of mean square contingency .013) between the rate of Court cases and the rate of Store arrests in the census areas of Chicago, the index of correlation being but .01.

If the residential distribution of the persons *arrested* by Lakeside Co. is different from the residential distribution of persons charged in the Municipal Court with shoplifting, is the distribution of the persons Lakeside Co. *formally charged* with shoplifting likewise different from the Municipal Court cases? Since Lakeside Co. prosecuted only 13 per cent of all adults arrested, there were too few cases to construct a rate map with these data alone. A spot map, however, showed in general the distribution of cases formally charged in the Municipal Court (Branch 40) by Lakeside Co. to be quite similar to that of all court cases and dissimilar to the Lakeside Co. arrest cases. Six of the seven areas with the highest number of court cases in the map of Lakeside Co. court cases are the same as the areas with the highest number of cases in Women's Court. Only three of these seven were among the top seven areas for actual Lakeside Co. arrests.

In addition to the records of Lakeside Co. obtained from the Store data, the data of the Municipal Court contained (for the three years studied) another sample of women (all the cases prosecuted in three years) charged with shoplifting by Lakeside Co. Since only 8.3 per cent of these cases duplicated the records of Lakeside Co. used in the Store data, the two samples could be combined to give a larger sample of the residential addresses of offenders prosecuted on the complaint of the Store. The two samples were thus combined and a map showing the rate of prosecuted women shoplifters per 1,000 female population (Map 4, p. 135)

Map 4. Residential addresses of women formally charged with shoplifting. Rate per 1,000 Chicago 1950 female population. N = 126

(Lakeside Co. Data)

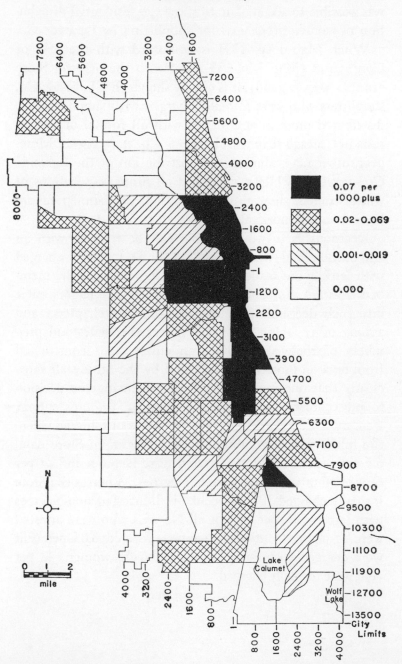

0.07 per 1000 plus

0.02-0.069

0.001-0.019

0.000

was constructed. This map combines as much data as it was possible to accumulate to show the residential distribution of women prosecuted for shoplifting by Lakeside Co.

When Map 4 (p. 135) is compared with the map of Court cases (Map 3, p. 133), and with the map for Store arrests (Map 1, p. 98), it is clearly shown that Lakeside Co. shoplifters who were *formally charged* with shoplifting are distributed more in accordance with all formal official arrests in Chicago than with Lakeside Co. store arrests. Moreover, other maps showing the distribution of the Lakeside Co. arrests of white women and all Store prosecutions of white women, show similar dispersion and similar failure to concentrate noticeably in any areas of the city.

Decisions as to which people will be released with an admonition and which people will be formally charged with larceny are made, as has been pointed out, by members of store protection staffs. A number of factors enter into such decisions (discussed in the first chapters) and among other factors, decisions reflect the biases and prejudices of these staffs. The residential maps constructed from data on prosecutions initiated by the Store staff show clearly that one important factor influencing the decision to prosecute is the race of the offender, for prosecutions were most frequent in the "ghetto" areas of Chicago where the inhabitants were almost totally Negro. In Store data, 6.5 per cent of all adults arrested were Negroes and 24 per cent of all prosecutions were of Negroes. Whereas the Store formally charged 10.9 per cent of all arrested non-Negroes with larceny, 58 per cent of all Negroes who were arrested were so charged. Of white women arrested 8.85 per cent were charged with larceny, and of Negro women, 42 per cent were formally charged.

Did the disproportionate charging of Negroes with larceny occur because the Negroes were "more criminal" than the whites? The median and mean values of merchandise which each group was recorded as having stolen was examined. Measured either by the median (since the distribution was skewed toward the upper values) or by the mean, Negro men and women arrested in the Store stole less valuable articles than white men and women so charged. It is clear that the magnitude of the crime was not the distinguishing factor. Roughly the same proportion of Negro and white women who were prosecuted had prior records (3/13 or 23 per cent of Negro women and 11/60 or 18 per cent of white women).

Table 4
Average Value in Dollars of Stolen Merchandise Found in the Possession of Adults Formally Charged, by Race and Sex
(Lakeside Co. Data)

	White	Negro
MEN		
Mean	71.00	32.70
Median	43.32	25.03
WOMEN		
Mean	46.86	25.03
Median	26.34	11.69

For Negro and white women in the Court sample, the difference between the number of objects stolen are very small at all age levels, and in no case is there statistical probability of a true difference.

Since being Negro was mainly equivalent at the time of this study in Chicago to residence in a "ghetto" area, the evidence thus indicates that a disproportionate number of people from these areas are brought to official attention through formal charges of larceny being placed against them. The same social forces, in other words, that operate to segregate people into the "ghettos," also operate to bring them to police and court attention. The Store arrest rate for shoplifting is much higher in many "good" residential areas than in deteriorated areas, but the proportion of people from these "good" residential areas who come to official attention is so small and the proportion of Negro "ghetto" dwellers brought to official attention so large that the reverse picture is seen in the Store cases which become part of official criminal statistics.

Moreover there is reason to believe that the reversal of proportions is true not only for the Lakeside Co. store arrests, but for all department store arrests. Store protection, as already noted, is a trade, and the practices which characterize this trade in one department store characterize it in others. If the selective processes are similar for all stores, and it seems probable that they are, an interesting figure can be derived which, *if* correct (and it is purely a hypothetical figure), could show the degree to which discrimination against Negro women affects the official criminal statistics on shoplifting by women.

For the Lakeside Co. data, the proportion of Negroes among women prosecuted is about 4 times the proportion found in women apprehended. Of Negro women, 13/31 or 42 per cent are prosecuted and 60/678 or 9 per cent of white women. Table 5 (p. 141) shows the number of Negro and white women officially charged with shoplifting for each of the Chicago stores which made official charges. The stores that would be expected to have the highest proportion of Negro women shoppers, i.e., stores carrying less expensive lines of merchandise, have a higher proportion of Negro women in their court prosecutions (Mandel, Fair, Sears, Wards, Goldblatts, Lerner) than do the "class" stores (Carson, Pirie, Scott; Marshall Fields; C. H. Stevens). Of Negro women, 349 were prosecuted, and 524 white women were prosecuted. If the proportion of white women arrested but not formally charged is four times the proportion of Negro women arrested but not charged as it is in the Lakeside Co. data then the relationship in store arrests is 4×524 or 2096 white women apprehended in store arrests to 349 Negro women. Thus 349/2445 or 14.2 per cent of all department store arrests of women, hypothetically, would be of Negro women. Since 7.9 per cent of the women 20 years of age and over in Chicago were, at the time of this study, Negro women, this would mean that Negro women were probably arrested in department stores about 1.8 times their proportion in the population instead of 4.5 times their proportion as appears in the official figures. It would also mean that the apparent concentration of cases of shoplifting in Negro "ghetto" areas was largely a direct result of minority group discrimination and not the result of a *real* rate of criminality among the people resident in those areas that much exceeds the rate in the nearby white residential areas.

The rate of arrest of Negro women is, even with the allowance for the screening procedures of stores, 1.8 times the rate for white women. It would seem probable that if an additional allowance could be calculated for the bias entering into the initial selection for arrest by store detectives, this proportion would be further reduced. An actual ratio of *crime* of 1 : 1 would not seem at all unlikely.

This study, presenting as it does, two sets of data ("official" and "private") on arrests for shoplifting gives an un-

usual opportunity to present a numerical analysis of racial
bias and discrimination. The question has, of course, been
raised many times before, but without answer. Sutherland,
for example, states:

The question which has been raised most persistently, perhaps,
is whether the arrests or juvenile court appearances do not give
a biased measure of delinquencies because of the poverty of the
families in the areas which are reported as having the highest
delinquency rates. Wealth and social position, to be sure, do
provide a certain degree of immunity against arrest. Also, certain
national or religious groups maintain welfare agencies which
take problem cases that would otherwise be referred to the police
or to the juvenile court, while other national and religious
groups have no agencies of this nature. *Even when allowance
is made for these variables,* the concentration seems to remain,
and this concentration is in accordance with the experience of
people who suffer from delinquencies. [Italics added.][7]

Sutherland's statement that "even when allowance is
made for these variables . . ." unfortunately gives no clue
as to how much allowance should be made. The allowance
which these department store data seem to indicate would,
in fact remove the extremely high concentration. Indeed
a "reasonable" allowance removes any concentration at all.

Does this discrimination factor apply only to shoplifting?
In this study there are no data on other types of crimes,
but since the judgment of whether or not a person is to
be officially charged with a crime has to be made by *someone* (private detective, employer, citizen, or policeman)
in most types of crime, it is probable that a very considerable allowance should be made for the existence of racial
prejudice in reporting other types of crime as well as shop-

7. Sutherland, Edwin H. *Principles of Criminology.* (Philadelphia,
1939), p. 139.

lifting and hence white and Negro actual crime rates for larceny by women at least are probably much closer than has been thought.

Table 5
Relation of Numbers of Negro and White Women Prosecutions for Shoplifting;

(Women's Court Data)

STORE	NEGRO		WHITE	TOTAL
	Number	Per cent		
Carson Pirie Scott	46	22.2	161	207
Mandel	72	49.6	73	145
Fair	46	63.9	26	72
Sears	26	48.2	28	54
Montgomery Ward	31	32.7	64	95
Marshall Field	11	15.5	60	71
Goldblatts	26	45.6	31	57
Lerner Shop	30	68.2	14	44
Robert Hall	10	71.2	4	14
Madigan	0	——	9	9
Wiebolts	0	——	3	3
C. H. Stevens	3	18.8	13	16
Lane Bryant	0	——	2	2
Spiegel	0	——	3	3
Boston	3	33.3	6	9
Other Clothing	31	78.4	9	40
Drug Stores	1	33.3	2	3
Variety Stores	8	66.7	4	12
Grocery Stores	5	29.4	12	17
Total	349	40.0	524	873

DISPOSITION OF CASES: STORE AND COURT

Store cases: After store officials have made the decision for disposition of a case, shoplifters are either "escorted" from the door with a warning never to return to the store, or they are formally charged and conveyed by the city police in a patrol wagon to the "lockup." Those that are to

be prosecuted are usually sent to jail for the night and
"booked"; when they can furnish or obtain bond, they are
released on bail until trial.

The typical trial averages 5 to 10 minutes and unless the
defendant has some sophistication in legal matters, the
trial is likely to be over before he realizes that it has begun.
In Women's Court especially, confused defendants were—
as I observed—propelled away from the judge's bench by
court aides or by their attorneys as they asked in a bewil-
dered way what was going to happen to them. And what
does happen to the shoplifter who is found guilty seemingly
depends on the sex, race, and prior record of the shoplifter,
and on the individual predilections of the judge who sits
on the bench.

Of the 110 *adults* from the Store sample who were formally charged with larceny, the outcome of court action
is known for 99. Of these 99, 43 per cent were sentenced to
jail for periods of from five days to one year; six per cent
were fined; 29 per cent were placed on probation; 21 per
cent were given token sentences ($1.00 considered paid and
one day considered served); and one was discharged without prosecution. None was found "not guilty." But the
overall figures conceal the differences found in court action
between sentences given to men and to women; to Negro
and to white shoplifters. Thirteen per cent of the white
women who were tried on the complaint of Lakeside Co.,
for example, were sentenced to jail, 33 per cent of the Negro women. Thus the likelihood of a Negro woman arrested
in the store serving a jail sentence is about six times the likelihood of a white woman (and keep in mind the similar
mean and median value of stolen merchandise as between
Negro women and white women). In proportion to their

numbers at time of apprehension, four times as many Negro women as white women were formally charged, and of those formally charged, twice as many Negro women were sentenced to jail.

Seventy per cent of white men tried were sentenced to jail and 75 per cent of Negro men. Men, as noted before, stole merchandise of greater value than women. They were also, in larger number than women, probably commercial thieves.

Court Cases: In the "Court sample" of women, differentials similar to those of the Store cases were found in sentences by racial group. Differences are especially striking in the proportions of Negro and white women not found guilty on the one hand, and those actually sentenced to jail on the other. Of white women 16.2 per cent were not found guilty and of Negro women 3.7 per cent (C.R. 6.7). Of white women, 4.1 per cent, and of Negro women 21.8 per cent were sentenced to jail (C.R. 7.46.) Of the 21 white women sentenced to jail, 2 (9.5 per cent) were sentenced for 30 days or more. Of the 76 Negro women, 20 (26.3 per cent) were sentenced for 30 days or more (C.R. 2.07). The differences in the proportion of jail sentences handed down to Negro and white women might have resulted from a greater proportion of commercial shoplifters or "occupational criminals" among Negro women. But, in the small sample of women whose prior court records were ascertained through Police Department records, of 15 white women sentenced to jail, 8 had prior records of arrest, and of 20 Negro women sentenced to jail, 10 had prior records.

The sentences imposed on women shoplifters by differ-

ent municipal court judges showed considerable variation.
Among eight judges who sat at the Women's Court in three
years, the range in the proportion of women found "not
guilty" ran from 5.0 per cent for one judge to 19.5 per cent
for another. Women given "token sentences" by judges
ranged form 0 for one judge to 58.4 per cent for another;
probation from 10.5 per cent to 62.4 per cent and jail
sentences ranged from 3.3 per cent to 31.2 per cent. The
idiosyncrasies of judges rotating in the same court have
been studied with similar conclusions by others.[8]

8. Smith R. H. and H. B. Ehrmann. *"The Criminal Courts,"* Cleve-
land Survey of Criminal Justice. Part 1, pp. 76–80. Also, Gaudet, F. J.,
G. S. Harris, and C. W. St. John. "Individual Differences in the Sentenc-
ing Tendencies of Judges," *Journal of Criminal Law, Criminology and
Police Science.* 23: 811–818, January, 1933.

CHAPTER VII

AN INTERPRETATION OF SHOPLIFTING

FROM THE DATA already presented, two points are fairly clear: shoplifting is a frequent crime; and most shoplifters are noncommercial pilferers.

Most shoplifting, including pilfering, appears to be chronic, habitual or systematic behavior. In substantiating this generalization, it may be well to summarize the evidence.

Sixty-one per cent of women in the store sample had more than one stolen object in their possession when arrested.

Only about 5–10 per cent of women detected in shoplifting are reported to have, when arrested, merchandise in their possession for which they had purchase receipts. It seems probable that a considerable section of the other 90–95 per cent were in the store intending to shoplift rather than to buy.

Most pilferers are reported by store detectives to have developed techniques for getting rid of price tags and other incriminating evidence; to have planned ways of evading detection; to have come to the store equipped with recep- tacles for stolen merchandise; to be alert to potential fol- lowers. With these evidences of sophistication in technique it appears impossible to think of these pilferers as impul- sive, accidental, or adventitious thieves.

There may or may not exist in any considerable number a third group of shoplifters consisting of impulsive persons who are overcome either by an unexpected urge to steal or an unpremeditated desire for a particular object. Occa- sional souvenir hunters are arrested by store police, but store protection personnel do not believe that these people repre- sent any important section of shoplifters either in numbers or certainly in their contribution to inventory shrinkage. Economically and residentially the data show that people who steal one object before being apprehended are not dif- ferent from other shoplifters.

Another generalization arising from the data presented is that most pilferers appear to have no present or sustained contact with a criminal subculture. Evidence on this point takes five forms.

(1) Ratios for the small selection sample of prosecuted shoplifters for whom prior records were obtained from the Police Department showed, when extrapolated to apply to the Court sample of adult women, that about 90 per cent of women who were officially charged with shoplifting had probably never before been convicted of any offense. Store data show that a maximum of two per cent of all women and 12 per cent of all men who were apprehended for shop- lifting had a prior criminal record with either private or public police in Chicago.

(2) Socioeconomic data on pilferers showed them to be

mainly "respectable" employed persons or equally "respectable" housewives.

(3) The residences of the Lakeside Co. pilferers in the city were not concentrated in slum areas, and neither were the residences of a sample of 407 white women whose addresses were obtained from the Court records and who had received "token" sentences or probation. Of this group, about 90 per cent (see No. 1 above) were persons who had probably never before been convicted of crime. Their residential distribution in Chicago was approximately that of the Lost and Found claimants of Lakeside Co., a measure presumed to be representative of typical shoppers in that store.

(4) The small value of the merchandise taken by pilferers implies that it could hardly have been stolen for sale to "fences" through recognized criminal channels. About 50 per cent of the women charged with shoplifting in the Court sample had been charged with stealing merchandise worth less than $14.95, and 15 per cent of the total had stolen less than $5.00 worth of merchandise. The actual median price tag values of merchandise stolen by persons arrested in the Store were $6.74 for adult women and $8.30 for adult men.

(5) Finally, the attitude of pilferers toward arrest may be cited as evidence of absence of contact with criminal subculture. In witnessing unobserved by the accused person, as the writer did, interrogations of arrested shoplifters, ignorance on the part of arrested pilferers of both criminal folkways and the actions of law enforcing agencies was only too obvious. Pilferers had no knowledge of arrest procedures, and they had clearly given little or no forethought to the consequences of their arrest. They appeared

to have thought about being "caught," but not about being *arrested*. Not understanding that they would be searched, for example, many attempted to give fictitious names (for a woman, usually her maiden name) while at the same time carrying a billfold or pocketbook with complete identification papers. (They did not realize that arrest implied search.) They consistently offered to pay for the stolen merchandise, failing to understand that they had been arrested and that the merchandise stolen had been impounded as evidence of theft and could not be bought by the thief. They frequently signed a waiver against suit of the store immediately after arrest—tantamount to a confession of guilt—but having signed the waiver, they talked threateningly about suit. (The waiver is simple in appearance saying that there has been no damage, physical or otherwise, at the hands of store personnel, and detailing possible physical damage. The "otherwise," of course, is the waiver against all suit.) Not infrequently pilferers confessed some of their past thefts to store detectives detailing the time, place, and objects stolen. Some of these past thefts had been memorable events arousing and continuing to arouse strong feelings of guilt.

These data seem to establish the fact that there exists a substantial number of persons who systematically steal merchandise usually for their own use and who are not in contact with a specific criminal subculture.

Although these persons were not, then, in association with law-violating groups, it is, however, possible and even probable that they had such associations in the past. Adult pilferers who work alone may have begun their careers as group juvenile delinquents, although not necessarily lower-class delinquents. It is apparent from the data that a large

number of young people in Chicago practice shoplifting
and presumably learn attitudes and rationalizations favorable to shoplifting and techniques for shoplifting in contact
with other adolescents. There is a steady and marked relationship between increasing chronological age and the
proportions of shoplifters arrested without companions or
accomplices. For women, especially, the number of cases
is sufficient to establish a trend, namely a steady and increasing proportion of persons arrested "alone" for each
5-year period between the ages of 15 and 65. The increase
of those alone when arrested is most marked between the
ages of 15 and 25. Year by year, there is an increase from
the ages of 9 to 19 of the proportion of shoplifters alone
when arrested. In five-year intervals, the range in the proportion "with others" when arrested runs from 100 per
cent for those less than nine years to 0 per cent for those
above 65 years of age. If indeed shoplifting is a form of
criminal behavior in which the techniques and supporting
attitudes are learned in the companionship of others, one
would expect to find decreasing evidence of companionship
as age increases, for at the younger age levels more people
would be in the initial stages of the learning process. This
is found, and found regularly and strikingly, in the proportion in which it would be expected. But the evidence on
the question is certainly incomplete. As far as the data
show, it is theoretically possible that the "group shoplifters" who are mainly juvenile may have ceased shoplifting on reaching maturity and a wholly different segment
of people began shoplifting in their mature years. It seems
more reasonable, however, to suppose that at least an important proportion of the juvenile pilferers either continued to shoplift or later restarted shoplifting.

Adult systematic or habitual pilferers, then, appear to be mainly "respectable" people not in contact with criminal subculture and showing no special knowledge of the adult criminal world. Although of adult age, pilferers' behavior when apprehended and their excuses for theft appear to be similar to the excuses of the juvenile group. The writer's impression was that in attempting to explain away their thefts, adult pilferers were using the lies, rationalizations, and alibis characteristic of children caught in acts considered reprehensible by adults. They were not realistically facing the different problem of being an arrested adult.

A further generalization from the data on shoplifting is that adult pilferers do not appear to be compulsive, neurotic personalities. Material bearing on the relationship of personality structure to shoplifting is as follows:

(1) Shoplifting is not frequently associated with psychoses of sufficient intensity to warrant commitment to a mental hospital. Only 12 of 873 or 1.4 per cent of women charged in the Court were committed to mental institutions; of the 1153 people in the Store sample, only four were committed, a rather smaller proportion, it would seem, than would be found in an unselected cross section of the population.

(2) Shoplifters were not found in psychiatric examination to have any consistent psychoneurotic patterns. Of the 873 women in the Court sample, 57 were recommended by the judges for psychiatric examination. Positive findings were recorded for 55. Of these, 12 (noted above) were committed to mental institutions. Of the remaining 43, eight were found to be suffering from involutional disturbances and this was the most frequent finding. No other single diagnosis was made for more than

six cases. Thus we can, say that no particular trend of personality aberration was recorded as characteristic of any considerable number of women shoplifters.

(3) Neither store arrests nor official charges indicate a tendency for shoplifting rates of women to increase during the ages (45–50) when menopause most frequently occurs.

(4) Among pilferers who are apprehended and interrogated by the store police but set free without formal charge, there is *very little or no recidivism*. This point, to be discussed later, is important in several respects and is relatively well established by the data of this study. The figures presented here on recidivism are in most respects more complete than "official" figures which are usually used. They include: 1) official figures of arrest by the Chicago Police Department for some cases; 2) the outcome of trial for a larger number of cases—an outcome, it has been established, based largely on known prior arrests; 3) the private arrest records cooperatively kept by the association for store protection maintained by ten downtown department stores in Chicago.

If shoplifting were a form of compulsive, neurotic, or irrational behavior (kleptomania), a very high rate of recidivism among pilferers would have been found. Few persons arrested for shoplifting ever receive the psychiatric attention necessary to alleviate deep-rooted personality disturbances. Yet, once arrested, interrogated, and in their own perspective, perhaps humiliated, pilferers apparently stop pilfering. The rate of recidivism is amazingly low. The reward of shoplifting, whatever it is, is not worth the cost to reputation and self-esteem. Pilfering is *not* for all, or almost all, shoplifters a basic neurotic manifestation in the sense that alcoholism or other compulsive behaviors seem to be. Even at great cost to their status and apparent comfort, alcoholics continue drinking. No compulsive neurotic ceases his neurotic behavior merely because he is told to do so no matter how forcibly he is told, but apparently shoplifting is a form of behavior which the person can govern apart from the general control of whatever psychoneurotic tendencies he may have.

It can be argued, and it may be a valid argument, that having been blocked from theft, emotionally disturbed persons merely find other ways of expressing hostile, antisocial, or compulsive behavior. Nevertheless if the focus of attention is on shoplifting specifically or even on criminality in general, the concrete direction taken by pathological impulses and the apparent modifiability of these directions is a matter of considerable practical importance. The housewife who has (hypothetically) had shoplifting as an outlet for hostility and finds after arrest that this outlet is now possible only at a greater risk to her reputation, self-esteem, and personal freedom than she is prepared to take, may turn to nagging her husband or she may develop an ulcer. To the psychotherapist whose goal is general personality adjustment, perhaps no essential change has been made. In the eyes of the law, the sociologist, or the store owner, however, the change has been very important, and the mechanism through which this change has been made needs to be understood as completely as possible.

SHOPLIFTING IN RELATION TO A THEORY OF CRIMINAL BEHAVIOR

In the interpretation of the causes of crime, sociologists have generally accepted some direct or modified form of cultural determinism. Psychologists have stressed crime as

a symptom of deeper emotional disturbance stemming from unmet needs in infancy and childhood or from uninhibited "id" impulses or similar sources deeply imbedded in the personality structure of the criminal.

The most widely accepted sociological viewpoint on the general sources of crime was placed directly by Sutherland when he constructed his theory of "differential association," stating:

Criminal behavior is learned . . . in interaction with other persons in a process of communication. . . . The principal part of the learning . . . occurs within intimate personal groups. . . . A person becomes delinquent because of an excess of definitions favorable to the violation of the law over definitions unfavorable to the violation of the law.[1]

Alexander and Staub give an equally direct statement of the psychoanalytical position.

Within the innermost nucleus of the personality . . . it is impossible to differentiate normal from criminal impulses. The human being enters the world as a criminal, i.e., socially not adjusted. During the first years of his life the human individual preserves his criminality to the fullest degree. . . . The criminal carries out in his actions his natural, unbridled, instinctual drives; he acts as the child would act if he could. The repressed, and therefore unconscious criminality of the normal man finds a few socially harmless outlets, like the dream and phantasy life, neurotic symptoms and also some transitional forms of behavior which are harmless. . . . The only difference between the criminal and the normal individual is that the normal man partially controls his criminal drives and finds outlets for them in socially harmless activities.[2]

1. Sutherland, Edwin H. *Principles of Criminology.* (Philadelphia, 1947), p. 4.
2. Alexander, Franz and Hugo Staub. *The Criminal, the Judge and the Public: A Psychological Analysis.* (New York), pp. 34–35.

The material on pilfering presented here constitutes an exception to narrowly defined cultural determinism, for in this study there have been isolated a substantial number of people who appear to be chronic, systematic thieves in the sense that their thefts are not unique, impulsive acts, but involve intent and planning and seem to be carried out with some frequency, regularity and sophistication; yet for these people there is no evidence of present association with criminal subculture, and there is, in fact, considerable evidence that there is no such association. Within the scope of this study there was no opportunity to discover whether or not individual pilferers had been associated with a delinquent subculture in the past. My own conjecture is that most of them had. In support of this belief may be cited the skills and techniques employed in shoplifting and the irresponsible and naive behavior of the arrested pilferers. The decreasing number of pilferers who were known to be "with others" at the time of arrest as the age of arrested pilferers increased also is relevant. It seems probable that having learned the arts and crafts of shoplifting from juvenile contemporaries, some adults continue pilfering by themselves and continue feeling that although they are adults they are, in fact, acting as naughty children and not really "criminal." Shoplifting thus appears to be the only crime in otherwise "blameless" lives. Adult pilferers are respectable people who carry on their criminal behavior clandestinely and surreptitiously.

The data on pilferers, then, appear to support the general psychiatric interpretation of crime presented earlier in the words of Alexander and Staub. Shoplifters act as children "would if they could." According to the data assembled here, pilferers do act like children, and a very large proportion of them *are* children. There is, however, more to the story than mere immaturity, either chronological or psychological. Pilfering is not just acting out unbridled, hostile "id" impulses. To understand pilfering we must know why hostile impulses are acted out by the very specific means of stealing merchandise from stores rather than by violence, crying, cringing or other possible outlets for hostile instinctual drives. Alexander and Staub's explanation is (and is intended to be) a general explanation of adult misbehavior. As such it can be an acceptable base on which to work. But the criminologist's question (and the storekeeper's as well) is "Why this particular outlet? Why shoplifting?"

Many psychiatrically oriented writers have attempted fairly specific explanations of pilfering. These explanations are uniformly disappointing because they are based on conjecture rather than evidence. Benjamin Karpman, Maslow and Mittlemann, and David Abrahamsen, among others, have stressed the belief that shoplifting belongs among the compulsive neurotic acts characteristic of sexually deprived and/or extremely hostile people.

The conditions grouped under the heading of manias are characterized by the fact that the patient engages in acts that are unlawful, in spite of the fact that he is reluctant to commit them and knows that he thereby runs the danger of arrest and punishment. Such patients behave and act well and apparently normally when they are not engaged in these activities. . . . The objects stolen are either not of much use to these individuals, or they do not have to be obtained through theft. . . . Sometimes a person steals objects which have a sexual significance for him. . . .[3]

3. Maslow, A. H. and Bela Mittlemann. *Principles of Abnormal Psychology*. (New York, 1941), p. 394.

Abrahamsen in his *Crime and the Human Mind* says,

> We are apt to be satisfied when it appears that a crime has been committed because of apparent gain, but this is not always the real motive. Indeed in delving into the causes of certain types of stealing, such as shoplifting . . . one finds motives which are beyond any comprehension of the culprit. One may find that stealing, which takes the form of a kleptomania, is an expression of a disguised wish for sexual intercourse. . . .
>
> In interpreting what takes place unconsciously in the mind of a pyromaniac or a kleptomaniac, one may say that desires of the id and a desire for punishment alternate, the obsessional neurosis acting as a defense against aggressive impulses. The conflict is internalized while the person's superego keeps the conflict back, with the result that he has to act out his inclination. Deep in the unconscious is a forbidden wish such as a sexual one.[4]

"The true kleptomaniac," says Karpman "belongs in the impulse-ridden and compulsive group. Female kleptomaniacs are believed to be sexually unsatisfied women with tremendous hostility."[5]

In several important respects the data in this study seem to be at variance with these psychological interpretations: (a) There are no data yet established to support the belief that shoplifting is particularly characteristic of women beyond the expected numbers implied in their presence as shoppers in places where shoplifting arrests are made. (b) The psychiatric data from Court cases present nothing to indicate the association of any substantial number of shoplifters with any recognized type of personality deviation. (c) The data show that pilferers generally take objects which are useful as status symbols rather than sexual

4. Abrahamsen, David. *Crime and the Human Mind*. (New York, 1944), pp. 21, 107.
5. Karpman, Benjamin, *The Sexual Offender and His Offenses*. (New York, 1954), p. 138.

symbols. (d) The data also indicate that once arrested, pilferers cease shoplifting. This fact is totally inconsistent
with the interpretation of shoplifting as "compulsive."
"There is never a repeat arrest of an individual who seemed
to realize his problems," said Edwards,[6] writing as an experienced store detective.

To find a case of "kleptomania," Edwards searched his
memory from the early part of his more than 20 years of
experience in store protection.

Probably the most typical case of kleptomania first came to
my attention shortly after entering protection work.

It was reported to me that an exceptionally well and expen-
sively dressed, distinguished and matronly-appearing woman
had been observed to steal several inexpensive articles. On two
other occasions she had attempted to secure refunds on items
for which she had no sales check; they were taken from her
and the refund refused. She made no further claim for them, so
instructions were given to the operators to apprehend her the
next time she lifted anything regardless of the price.

Within a few days she was caught stealing items with a value
of about $12.00. She admitted previous thefts and gave assur-
ance that it would never occur again. She was advised to discuss her problem with her husband, a man of prominence.

Several months later she was again apprehended shoplifting.
On this occasion she dropped to her knees and begged and
pleaded that her husband should not be called. Anything would
be promised to avoid it. He was called.

The husband was critical of the fact that he had not been
notified of the first episode because he had subsequently been
embarrassed when she had taken something from the home of
friends. I was blamed for his embarrassment over this, but
after some discussion the couple left to visit a psychiatrist.

Some time later I learned that the same woman had been

6. Edwards, Loren. *Shoplifting and Shrinkage Protection for Stores.*
(Springfield, Ill., 1958), p. 135.

taken to court for shoplifting in another store but that was not her last experience.

Some months elapsed and she was once more apprehended, and again was taken to court. Her psychiatrist appeared in court at the time of this trial, and informed the judge that the defendant had refused to cooperate with his efforts at treatment and had been sent to a sanitarium by her husband. While there she had pilfered articles from the rooms of other patients which caused her dismissal.

I credit the judge with a wise decision. He continued the case for one year with the stipulation that she was to cooperate with the doctor; that if she failed to do so he was to report to the court, her case would then be advanced on the docket, and she would be sentenced to serve a year's term. The doctor gave a favorable report and she was discharged when the case was finally heard a year later.

I chanced to meet this woman once since. She was in the store with a friend but stopped to assure me that she had overcome her problems and would never again meet me under the previous circumstances. This last meeting was many years ago and I am confident that if she had been in any trouble since, that is, in our city, I would have heard of it.[7]

Although neither conventional sociological explanations of career criminality nor explanations of shoplifting as a consequence of psychological disturbance seem to fit the data, some hypotheses, however, can be put forward which do fit the research data. These hypotheses can be rephrased in more general terms, and the relationship of the findings on pilfering to other research data discussed. In the final chapter, and going beyond the hypotheses on shoplifting, some speculation will be made in an effort to relate the data on pilfering to a more general theory of criminal behavior.

7. Edwards, *Ibid.*, pp. 52–53.

EXPLANATION OF PILFERING

It seems probable that most adult pilferers start their careers as children or adolescents in groups where the techniques of successful pilfering are learned from other more experienced children. Later as group activity is abandoned some of the group members continue the practices they learned as adolescents. The lavish displays of merchandise which department stores exhibit to encourage "impulse buying" are, for the experienced pilferer, there for the taking.

Adult women pilferers, generally belonging to families of rather modest income, enter department stores with a strong sense of the limitations of their household budgets. They do not steal merchandise which they can rationalize purchasing: household supplies, husband's clothes, children's wear. But beautiful and luxury goods for their personal use can be purchased legitimately only if some other member of the family is deprived. Although pilferers often have guilt feelings about their thefts, it still seems to them less wrong to steal from a rich store than to take from the family budget. Pilferers seem to be, thus, narcissistic individuals in that they steal for their own personal use, but, on the other hand, they do not use the limited family income for their own luxury goods.

Pilferers differ in one outstanding respect, at least, from other thieves: They generally do not think of themselves as thieves. In fact, even when arrested, they resist strongly being pushed to admit their behavior is theft. This became very clear as I observed a number of interrogations of shoplifters by the Store detective staff, and it was supported in conversations with the detectives who drew on their own wider experience. It is quite often difficult for the store staff to convince the arrested person that he has actually been arrested, even when the detectives show their licenses and badges. Again and again store police explain to pilferers that they are under arrest as thieves, that they will, in the normal course of events, be taken in a police van to jail, held in jail until bond is raised, and tried in a court before a judge and sentenced. Much of the interview time of store detectives is devoted to establishing this point; in making the pilferer understand that what happens to him from the time of his arrest is a legal question, but it is still a question for decision, first of all, by the store staff.

Store detectives use the naivete of pilferers as an assistance in arrest procedures while the pilferer is in the presence of legitimate customers on the floor of the store. The most tactful approach possible is used. The store detective will say, for example, "I represent the store office, and I'm afraid the office will have to see what's in your shopping bag. Would you care to come with me, please?" If the pilferer protests, the detective adds, "You wouldn't want to be embarrassed in front of all these people, would you? In the office we can talk things over in private."

Edwards states that the method of making an arrest is important in preventing excitement and even disorder.

A gentle approach will usually disarm any shoplifter, amateur or professional, while a rough seizure or loud accusation may immediately put him on the defensive. At other times it may result in a nervous or hysterical condition accompanied by an involuntary discharge which may be embarrassing to both the arrestor and the arrested.[8]

8. Edwards, *Ibid.*, p. 134.

Inbau adds the thought that the gentle approach is helpful too in forestalling suits for false arrest.

The finesse with which defendant accosts plaintiff is a definite factor also affecting the temper with which the court approaches a case. The defendant acting in good faith with probable cause, whose attitude is quiet, non-threatening, and deferential to the plaintiff's feelings can weather an honest mistake much more cheaply than otherwise. At the most it may induce a court to find there was no imprisonment at all. At the least, it will relieve defendant of punitive damages and reduce the amount of actual damages.[9]

The "deference" of the arresting detective combined with the already existing rationalizations of the pilferer sustain in him the belief that whereas his behavior might be reprehensible, the objects taken were, after all, not of great value; he would be glad to pay for them and be on his way. "Yes, I took the dress," one woman sobbed as she was being closely interrogated, "but that doesn't mean I'm a thief."

Arrest forces the pilferer to think of himself as a thief. The interrogation procedure of the Store is specifically and consciously aimed at breaking down any illusions the shoplifter may have that his behavior is regarded as merely "naughty" or "bad." The breakdown of illusions is, to the store detective staff, both a goal in itself and a means of establishing the fact that each innocent-appearing pilferer, is not in fact, a professional thief "putting on an act." In the interrogation the shoplifter is searched for other stolen merchandise and for identification papers. Pockets and pocketbooks are thoroughly examined. All papers, letters, tickets, bills, etc., are read in detail in spite of con-

9. Inbau, Fred E. "Protection and Recapture of Merchandise from Shoplifters," *Illinois Law Review*. Vol. 46, No. 6, 1952.

siderable protest from the arrested person. Each person is made to explain everything he has with him. If suspect items such as public locker keys, pawn tickets, etc., are found, he will have to explain very thoroughly indeed and agree to have the locker examined and the pawned merchandise seen to avoid formal charge. In any event, once name, address, and occupation have been established (and for women, the maiden name and names in other marriages), the file of names and identifying material of all persons who have, in the past years, been arrested in any of the State Street department stores is consulted. The shoplifter is questioned at length if similarities of names or other identifying data are encountered.

While identification and prior record are being checked, store detectives, persons in charge of refunds, and even experienced sales clerks may be summoned to look at the arrested person to determine if he has been previously suspected of stealing merchandise or has been noted as behaving suspiciously.

In the course of all this investigation, it becomes increasingly clear to the pilferer that he is considered a thief and is in imminent danger of being hauled into court and publicly exhibited as such. This realization is often accompanied by a dramatic change in attitudes and by severe emotional disturbance. Occasionally even hysterical semi-attempts at suicide result.

The professional shoplifter who has been arrested and knows he is recognized, on the other hand, behaves quite differently. He does, of course, make every effort possible to talk his way out of the situation. But once he finds that this is impossible, he accepts jail and its inconveniences as a normal hazard of his trade.

"This is a nightmare," said one woman pilferer who had been formally charged with stealing an expensive handbag. "It can't be happening to me! Why, oh why can't I wake up and find that it isn't so," she cried later as she waited at a store exit, accompanied by a city and a store policeman, for the city police van to arrive. "Whatever will I do? Please make it go away," she pleaded with the officer. "I'll be disgraced forever. I can never look anyone in the face again."

Pilferers expect no "in-group" support for their behavior. As they become aware of the possible serious consequences of their arrest (trial, jail, etc.), pilferers obviously feel isolated from all supporting relationships. Store detectives report that the most frequent question women ask is, "Will my husband have to know about this?" Men, they say, express immediate fear that their employers will be informed of their arrest when questions about employment are raised. Children are apprehensive of parental reaction. Edwards says,

The composure of juveniles being detained has never ceased to amaze me, that is, until notified that they must tell a parent of their misdemeanor. Then the tears flow and pleadings begin. The interviewer must be firm in his denial that notification will "kill" the parent, and he must sell the child on the idea that any deviation from accepted practice must be discussed with the person most interested in his welfare.[10]

Pilferers feel that if their family or friends learn about their arrest they will be thoroughly disgraced. The fear, shame, and remorse expressed by arrested pilferers could not be other than genuine and a reflection of their appraisal of the attitudes they believe others will take toward them. One

10. Edwards, *Op. cit.*, pp. 135–136.

woman was observed who, thoroughly shaken as the realization of her predicament began to appear to her, interrupted
her protestations of innocence from time to time, over-
whelmed at the thought of how some particular person in
her "in-group" would react to her arrest. Her conversation with the interrogator ran somewhat as follows: "I
didn't intend to take the dress. I just wanted to see it in
daylight. [She had stuffed it into a shopping bag and carried it out of the store.] Oh, what will my husband do? I
did intend to pay for it. It's all a mistake. Oh, my God,
what will my mother say! I'll be glad to pay for it. See,
I've got the money with me. Oh, my children! They can't
find out I've been *arrested!* I'd never be able to face
them again."

Pilferers not only expect no in-group support, but they
feel that they have literally *no* one to turn to. The problem
of being embroiled in a wholly unfamiliar legal situation is obviously not only frightening but unexpected. Apparently they had anticipated being reprimanded; they
had not anticipated being searched by a licensed detective,
identified, etc., and on the whole, placed in a position in
which the burden of argument for keeping out of jail is
theirs.

The contrast in behavior between the pilferer and the
recognized and self-admitted thief is striking. The experienced thief either already knows what to do or knows precisely where and how to find out. His emotional reactions
may involve anger directed at himself or at features in the
situation around him, but he is not at a loss for reactions.
He follows the prescribed modes of behavior, and knows,
either because of prior experience or through the vicarious
experiences of acquaintences, what arrest involves by way

of obligations and rights. He has some familiarity with bonding practice and either already has or knows how to find a lawyer who will act for him.

Because the adult pilferer does not think of himself, prior to his arrest, as a thief and can conceive of no in-group support for himself in that role, his arrest forces him to reject the role (at least insofar as department store shoplifting is concerned). The arrest procedure, even though not followed by prosecution, is in itself sufficient to cause him to redefine his situation. He is, of course, informed that subsequent arrest by any store will be followed by immediate prosecution and probably by a considerable jail sentence. But since this does not act as a deterrent to the self-admitted thief nor could this kind of admonition deter the compulsive neurotic, neither the fear of punishment nor the objective severity of the punishment in itself is the crucial point in relation to the change from criminal to law abiding behavior. Rather the threat to the person's system of values and prestige relationships is involved. Social scientists who have investigated criminal activities which have subcultural support are unanimous in pointing out the persistence of criminal activity; the high rate of recidivism and the resistance to reform shown by law violators. Pilfering seems to be the other side of the coin. Not having the support of a criminal subculture, pilferers are very "reformable" individuals. If the findings of this study are substantiated by studies of other offenses in which the offenders are similarly without support of a criminal subculture, there would be a strong argument in favor of keeping pilferers out of jail lest they receive there the kinds of knowledge and emotional support they need to become "successful" commercial thieves. Crime prevention

would seem best achieved by helping the law violators re-
tain their self-image of respectability while making it clear
to them that a second offense will really mean disgrace.

Cloward and Ohlin give much weight to this point when
discussing juvenile offenders:

The youngster who is motivated by a sense of injustice generally commits his first acts of defiance in a climate of uncer-
tainty and fear of disapproval. The withdrawal of attributions
of legitimacy from the dominant social norms is initially tentative and unstable. These first acts are usually minor and often
impulsive expressions of resentment against the apparent injustice of the established social order. However, they bring the
individual into conflict with the official system and expose him
to its arsenal of invidious definitions and punitive sanctions.
Members of the conventional community are likely to respond
to them with strong efforts at repression, precisely because they
recognize the underlying attitude of alienation from the established norms. These early acts of defiance are in effect tentative steps toward the adoption of norms in competition with the
official rules. At this stage the deviant needs all the encouragement he can muster to defend his position. He finds these by
searching out others who have faced similar experiences and
who will support one another in common attitudes of alienation from the official system.[11]

The first offender, whether juvenile or adult, need not
search far to find others who have faced similar experiences
if he is placed in an institution populated wholly by others
who have similarly been arrested.

Generalizing from the data of this study we find:

A. Some forms of criminal behavior can be carried on
in isolation from supporting relationships for the activities

11. Cloward, Richard and Lloyd Ohlin. *Delinquency and Opportunity.*
(New York, 1960), pp. 126–127.

of the law violator, but in such a noncriminal system of relationships and values, criminal behavior is unstable and ceases when the person finds that to continue the behavior he must define himself as a criminal with the consequent status changes.

1. This means that it is possible for a person to behave as a thief without defining himself as a thief and without seeing his behavior as it will be defined by representatives of the law enforcing culture.

2. On the other hand, it is possible for a person to behave as a thief and to accept himself as a thief when it does not isolate him from his primary group and community contacts. This, of course, is a characteristic of the "booster" and is apparently the common condition in most other kinds of recognized delinquency and crime (burglary, confidence games, robbery, pocketpicking, the "protected" rackets, etc.).

3. When, however a person is unwilling to accept himself as a thief because it will isolate him from his intimates (he will lose his "respectability"), he will cease stealing. He will cease even though his satisfaction from the crimes has been great, his motivation to continue his theft has been strong, his emotional adjustment weak, his psychological reaction apparently compulsive, or inadequate and infantile, or "he" is a woman suffering from an involutional reaction.

Since most shoplifters do not conceive of themselves as thieves, how do they perceive their own behavior? On this very interesting question the statistical data provide little information. The only clues we have are in the kinds of merchandise taken, which has been commented upon, and from the scattered interview material. Pilferers appear to take merchandise just a little above the level of that which they would buy and they rationalize their thefts so that their behavior can appear to themselves as somewhat reprehensible but not really criminal. They steal, for example, at stores which carry inexpensive lines of merchandise, and even at Lakeside Co., many shoplifters steal from the "budget floor."

Exactly what the rationalizations are, how frequently different types of rationalizations are used could not be determined from the evidence available in this study. An examination of the psychological mechanisms used by pilferers to explain their crimes to themselves and to others would be very interesting.

Pilfering is not the only form of criminal behavior, however, in which processes of rationalization seem to operate in a similar way. Cressey found in his study of embezzlement that

. . . trusted persons become trust violators when they conceive of themselves as having a financial problem which is non-shareable, have the knowledge or awareness that this problem can be secretly resolved by violation of the position of financial trust, and are able to apply to their own conduct in that situation verbalizations which enable them to adjust their conceptions of themselves as users of entrusted funds or property.[12]

Cressey found further,

. . . most of the trust violators encountered did not so much abandon the folkways of legitimate business behavior as they did restructure the situation in such a way that, from their point of view, they were not abandoning the folkways. Similarly, except for the absconders, the attitudes of the men interviewed

12. Cressey, Donald. "The Criminal Violation of Financial Trust," *American Sociological Review*, 1950, p. 742.

were not so much "anti-social" as they were "pro-social" in that the endeavor was to keep from considering themselves as criminals.[13]

Cressey quote numerous statements of different embezzlers who behaved in a criminal manner without so defining themselves.

I did not plan to keep the money permanently, though I never thought much about just how I was going to get it back.

If the rural depression, which was already bad in that year had ended the next year, I could have replaced the bonds and no one would have known the difference. . . . I have never felt that I was committing a crime.

Maybe it was phony reasoning but I was going to put it [the money] back. . . .

On the embezzlement, in my way of thinking, it wasn't embezzlement because I was borrowing it. . . .

I reasoned that I was going to pay it back ($150) in three or four days, and I did pay it back. In a matter of a few days I took some more—it got easier as time went on. From then on it varied. There might be a period of a week or ten days when I'd neither put in nor take out.[14]

Cressey also pointed out that there was a different group of embezzlers, not included in his study, who were, in fact, confidence men or other professional criminals who obtained positions of trust under false pretenses for the purpose of theft. These appear similar to "boosters."

There is unquestionably much in the common culture to support theft, especially petty theft. Most people with whom I have discussed the problem admit to having

13. Cressey, Donald. *The Criminal Violation of Financial Trust.* (Unpublished dissertation, Indiana University), p. 132.
14. *Ibid.*, pp. 85–110.

stolen items of small value. Sutherland found among his
university classes that 98 per cent of the students were at
least "mildly delinquent"[15] and an examination of a part
of his original data showed that 20 of 36 (55 per cent) of
the students admitted shoplifting, chiefly from variety
stores. Some of them recorded as rationalization for their
thefts that stores were rich and the little they took "would
never be missed." It seems likely that this might be a type of
rationalization commonly used by pilferers.

Going beyond the concrete conclusions from Cressey's
data on embezzlers and from the data of this study, certain
speculations on broader aspects of criminological theory
can be suggested.

15. *Op. cit.*, p. 113.

CHAPTER VIII

THE "RESPECTABLE" CRIMINAL
AND THE YOUNG OFFENDER

BEFORE CONSIDERING some of the conclusions
which grow directly out of this study, it may be well to
point out the obvious but easily forgotten fact that certain
kinds of theft are an integral part of an acquisitive society,
especially a society resting on an economic base of corporate enterprise. In the anonymity of urban life, possession of the outward symbols of success is often equated
with achievement and is essential to upward social mobility. Social status is symbolized by the ownership of personal property: smart clothes, this year's car, a good house.

In department stores many of these symbols of status
are dazzlingly arrayed before people who have been ex-
horted to desire them. Manufacturers employ skilled professional tempters (advertising agencies) to represent their
products as necessary ingredients for the appearance of
success. Small wonder, then, that businesses which reap the
profits of acquisitiveness also suffer the by-product: theft.

When an abundance of highly attractive consumer goods
is displayed on the open shelves of relatively unguarded

stores, and when low-paid employees daily handle millions
of dollars in money belonging to impersonal corporations,
it is inevitable that a certain proportion of people will try
to obtain merchandise or money by the simple and direct
method of appropriation. Together, the impersonality of
the corporation and the needs of the middle class, family
oriented man or woman combine into an atmosphere con-
ducive to rationalized theft; snitches, embezzlers, and "till-
tappers" alike come out of the acquisitive corporate society; and so, too, though through somewhat different
processes, do boosters, other professionals, and the criminal
subculture which nourishes them.

Further research is clearly needed into the origins and supporting milieu for the crimes of "respectable" people. One
may speculate that the status-oriented middle-class value
structure and the *anomie* of organized society are themselves relevant factors. Increasingly people work for, buy
from, and administer the affairs of impersonal corporations.
People who would never consider stealing articles from a
friend's home or even from the "corner" grocer may have
very different feelings about stealing merchandise displayed for sale in a branch of a large retail chain store.
Someone who would be scrupulous about returning borrowed money to a friend can rationalize till-tapping from
an employing organization, especially if he believes that the
executives above him are taking bribes, padding their ex-
pense accounts, or otherwise "getting their cuts."

Advertising appeals, merchandise display practices, and
deferred payments encourage the middle-class employee to
live on *next* year's income (which hopefully will be larger
than this year's) and to maintain his family and himself at
a more opulent level than he can afford. The strongly
family-centered value system of the middle class and the

vicarious enjoyment parents receive from the upward social mobility of their children combine to create insistent financial needs that cannot be met by current earnings.

Cohen, and Cloward and Ohlin have expressed rather forcefully the concept that juvenile delinquency arises in situations of frustration for the achievement of middle-class goals.

We believe that deviance and conformity generally result from the same kinds of social conditions. As Cohen has pointed out: People are prone to assume that those things which we define as evil and those which we define as good have their origins in separate and distinct features of society. Evil flows from poisoned wells; good flows from pure and crystal fountains. The same sources cannot feed both. Our view is different. The idea that deviance and conformity can arise from the same features of social life is based on a further assumption; that efforts to conform, to live up to social expectations, often entail profound strain and frustration. . . . Thus efforts to be what one is supposed to be sometimes leads to aberrant behavior. Reaching out for socially approved goals under conditions that preclude their legitimate achievement may become a prelude to deviance. Conformity, taking cultural mandates seriously, is thus a crucial step in the process by which deviance is generated.[1]

The data on shoplifting, with their indication of a strong middle-class component, point to a similar conclusion. The middle class itself cannot always achieved middle-class goals by legitimate means. The frustration is not so profound as in the lower class, however, and the individual thefts of middle-class people are sometimes of small magnitude, but middle-class people do try theft as a means to bridge the gap between earnings and "needs" and many of them are at least temporarily successful.

Present day society being what it is, then, it is apparent

1. Cloward, R. A. and L. E. Ohlin. *Delinquency and Opportunity.* (New York, 1960), pp. 37–38.

that even excellent police-work, within a business enterprise, cannot prevent all theft. All it can do is to make it
more difficult to steal. Private police aim only at setting
up effective preventive practices and apprehending some of
the thieves. Their functions, however, as we have already
noted, present special problems for the criminologist. How
extensive these are seems to be little realized.

PRIVATE POLICE

In gross numbers of people apprehended for all forms of
larceny, in fact, private police may equal or possibly exceed
the numbers of arrests of public police. It is important to
consider the broader implications of the functions of private police both for this reason and because their unrecorded actions create major distortions in criminal statistics. And criminal statistics are the basic data on which
theories of crime causation are built. The selective opera-
tions of private police in prosecuting some people and dis-
missing others with a warning introduce, as I have indicated,
several major distortions into statistics compiled about the
criminal population. In his *White Collar Crime* Sutherland
developed as his central thesis that:

. . . persons of the upper socio-economic class engage in much
criminal behavior; that this criminal behavior differs from the
criminal behavior of the lower socio-economic class principally
in the administrative procedures which are used in dealing
with offenders; and that variations in administrative procedures
are not significant from the point of view of causation of crime.[2]

Not only "persons of respectability and high social
status," as Sutherland defined white collar criminals—he

2. Sutherland, Edwin H. *White Collar Crime.* (New York, 1949), p. 9.

was writing mainly of business men—commit crimes, but as the data of this study suggest, many "respectable" persons of lesser social status also commit crimes which are processed through para-official agencies, and which, in consequence, fail to become part of the public record.

Private police, as noted in the early part of this study, are widely employed by business firms for the prevention of theft, in the apprehension of thieves, and in the detection of fraud, embezzlement, larceny, and other crimes. They are regularly employed not only by department stores but by hotels, industrial plants, retail grocery and drug stores. In hotels, and probably in other settings as well, private police are employed in part to protect offenders from public attention. Drunk and disorderly persons, sex offenders and even known professional thieves are kept "under cover" to protect the good name of the institution.

Banks, railways, insurance companies, manufacturers, and bonding companies use the services of private police as do most commercial enterprises whenever a relationship of "trust" must be established between employer and employee. In most occupations any relationship of trust implies prior investigation of each trusted employee and a continuing check of his trustworthiness.

John Bartlow Martin, who knows the field well, wrote on the functions of private detectives:

Of course private detectives sometimes catch criminals. But an agency which uncovers an arson conspiracy while working for an insurance company is more interested in voiding the arsonist's insurance claim than in jailing him. Similarly the prime objective of a private detective who tracks down a jewel thief is to retrieve the jewels. If an agency unmasks a dishonest bank clerk, the bank, rather than prosecute him, simply gets its money back and fires him. . . . Many detective agencies provide plant guards and patrolmen. Others make what are called "personnel surveys" in stores, hotels, night clubs, restaurants, banks, and transportation systems. In plainer words they find out how much the employees are stealing. Some detectives check on job applicants, some make credit reports, or investigate personal injury claims for insurance companies and common carriers.[3]

Embezzlement, fraud, and larceny are certainly underrepresented in conventional criminal statistics, because these are the crimes for which private police are frequently employed to apprehend the culprit. Sex offenses, disorderly conduct, and public intoxication are also underrepresented for the same reason. To repeat the questions posed before: How many employees, executive and otherwise, steal from their employers? How frequent are attempts to deceive insurance companies? How many people abscond to avoid repayment of borrowed money? How frequently, for that matter, are adulteries committed in hotel rooms? How often do tradesmen and professional workers deceive customers, patients, and clients for personal benefit? At present all we can say is—as newspaper reports alone suffice to show—these crimes are frequent.

The underrepresentation of embezzlement, fraud, and larceny in conventional criminal statistics means an underrepresentation of the "respectable middle class" among the offenders. Re-emphasizing a point already made, one must be respectably established in the community as an employed adult to borrow money from a private institution or even to obtain merchandise through installment buying. Larceny from an employer obviously implies employment. Being a skilled tradesman or professional person in private

3. Martin, John Bartlow. "*Peekaboo Pennington, Private Eye,*" *Harper's*. May, 1946, pp. 450–461.

employment is likewise an index of middle-class status. It is apparent that the thought has now to be entertained that a comprehensive examination of all private and public records of crime in an urban area might reveal that instances of crime are spread rather evenly throughout the social classes of the population. Such examination would almost certainly show, however, that the kinds of delinquencies would differ as the social class backgrounds of offenders differ. Some kinds of delinquent and criminal behavior seem to be generated in the subcultures of the slums. Other kinds apparently originate among those who live in middle-class residential areas.

Although the work of private police has been largely overlooked by sociologists, this does not mean that it must continue to be overlooked. Private police keep excellent records. With proper safeguards for anonymity these records can be made available to the legitimate research worker.

The failure of sociologists to include the crimes carried out by business men in the course of their businesses, has resulted, Edwin H. Sutherland pointed out in his book *White Collar Crime*, in (a) an underestimation of the amount of crime; (b) a distortion of the relative frequencies of different types of crime; and (c) a biased view of the personal characteristics of law violators. Failure to include the data of private police has exactly the same consequence.

Amount of crime. The exclusive use of public records as data on criminal behavior has resulted in a considerable underestimation of the amount of crime and of the number of law violators.

Of all arrests made in Lakeside Company for shoplifting,

for example, only 12 per cent came to official attention through formal charges being placed against the shoplifters. Eighty-eight per cent of arrested shoplifters (and these predominantly middle-class white women) did not appear in public records at all.

In 1944, Lakeside Co. arrested approximately 360 adult women for shoplifting; in 1945, 420. In these years the Chicago Police Department reported that 426 (1944) and 636 (1945) adult women were formally charged with larceny of *all* forms (including shoplifting) in the City of Chicago. The arrests in one store of adult women shoplifters (88 per cent of which were unreported to the police) were in 1944 and again in 1945 about two-thirds as frequent as were the arrests of adult women for all forms of larceny recorded by the entire city police department.

Although shoplifting is one of the largest categories of arrest by Store police, it is not, as we have noted, the only charge on which people are arrested in department stores. Some store employees are arrested as thieves and embezzlers. Pickpockets, purse-snatchers, disorderly persons, sex offenders, and other law violators are also apprehended by store police. Many offenders in all categories are not brought to official notice.

Moreover, the protection department of Lakeside Co. has a very small staff compared to the total staff membership of the many private agencies of law enforcement in Chicago. And other private agencies similarly are reluctant to use their protection personnel in the lengthy process of prosecution. Sutherland stated that in a "short consecutive series of embezzlements known to a surety company, 90 per cent were not prosecuted because prosecution would have interfered with restitution or salvage. The evidence in cases of embezzlement is generally conclusive, and would probably have been sufficient to justify conviction in all the cases in the series."[4]

Types of crime. Failure to consider adequately the operation of private agencies of law enforcement not only minimizes the total number of crimes and of criminals but also (an even more serious matter for criminological theory) distorts the relative frequency of different types of crimes. The frequency of shoplifting has certainly been underestimated, and since employee theft is usually handled by private police also, it is certain that the number of crimes (stealing of money, merchandise, tools and equipment) committed by employed persons in the course of their employment is likewise considerably underestimated. On the other hand, types of theft which are handled directly by public police (armed robbery, for example) appear much more prominently than is warranted. How large the amount of privately handled crime is, or how seriously its absence in the published criminal statistics distorts the total body of criminological data can, until further research is conducted, merely be conjectured. Perhaps, like an iceberg, the largest proportion of crime is kept below the surface.

Personal characteristics of law violators. The material on shoplifting showed that a private police system acts as a screening agency because only some and not all of its arrests are officially reported. The nature of the selective process for arrested shoplifters minimized, at least, the number of white people, middle class people, and women, especially older women who come to official attention.

4. Sutherland, Edwin H. "White Collar Criminality," *American Sociological Review*. Vol. V, pp. 1–12, 1940.

Data were presented showing selection by age, race, and residential distribution. Available data were often insufficient to analyze the entire selective process, but where data were sufficient, the following results can be summarized:

Age. Shoplifting has very little age limitation. It is "open" both to children and to adults, and children are detected shoplifting in disproportionate numbers (even in downtown department stores) to their percentages in the population. Store data show that women age 65 and over continue to shoplift with about the same rate in proportion to their numbers in the population as women 25–40. They are, however, seldom charged in court, but neither are they "little old ladies" who are allowed to shoplift as they wish.

Shoplifting, however, is probably one of the few crimes handled by private police which is "open" to juveniles. Most crimes investigated by private police are crimes of adults. When the victim of a crime is the *employer*, the law violator must be an *employed* adult. Thus all private police records taken together are probably disproportionately criminal records of employed people (just as public police records are disproportionately those of unemployed people). It would be interesting and important to know more about adults who have *not* been juvenile offenders (who have led "blameless lives"), but who commit crimes in the course of their employment. This is but one of the problems that obviously needs investigation, but it is beyond the scope of the present study.

Race. Negro women comprised 4.4 per cent of all women arrested in Lakeside Co. They comprised 17.8 per cent of all women officially charged by the store. Only 8.8 per cent of white women arrested by the store police were officially charged, but 42 per cent of Negro women were officially charged. This difference in proportions is not a result of thefts of greater magnitude by Negro women nor of a greater proportion of Negro women with prior criminal records.

In the Court cases presented, Negro women are found to be charged by the stores with shoplifting about four to five times as frequently as white women in proportion to their numbers in the city population. But if the proportions of arrests-to-charges, by race, that obtains in Lakeside Co. holds for other stores as well, Negro women are only arrested by stores 1.8 times their proportion in the population, and this proportion may well result from the selective observations of store detectives.

If additional *private* police records were available not only for shoplifting in both department and specialty stores but also for theft by employess in businesses of all kinds, what would be the racial distribution of law violators and what proportion turned over to the police? At the time the data of this study were collected, few Chicago firms employed Negro people in positions as sales clerks, cashiers, tellers, accountants, or in other occupations in which they handled financial transactions. A full accounting of employee theft would necessarily show a picture of arrest by race (and age and sex) very different from that conventionally given in research monographs and textbooks on criminology.

Residential distribution. Residential spotmapping of Women's Court cases showed a high concentration of shoplifters in the slum and Negro "ghetto" areas. There is no similar finding for the residences of persons arrested for shoplifting at Lakeside Co. The residence map of women *formally charged* by the Store, however, shows a concentration similar to that of all Women's Court cases. The hypothesis that appears evident is that the same prejudice and discrimination that segregates racial and other minorities into slum and "ghetto" areas operates also to bring them to official attention when they are involved in law violations.

PILFERING, BOOSTING, AND THEORIES OF CRIME CAUSATION

Although pilferers are by no means the only category of offenders whose records are, for the most part, kept in the files of private police and not made part of public data, they are a particularly significant group. If most pilferers are indeed respectable people who are neither in contact with criminal subcultures nor are compulsive-neurotic personalities, their existence is significant from the general viewpoint of criminology. Since they do not appear to conform to any theoretical expectation, their presence indicates some need to modify existing theory.

In suggesting a possible modification, it is useful to view pilfering as one illustration of a broader category of crime which we shall call incidental or *peripheral crime,* in contrast to *vocational crime.* Other numerous groups of the criminal population remain outside either of these categories. They include, for example, people who are arrested on charges such as "drunk and disorderly", vandalism, sex offenses, assault and battery, reckless driving, homicide, criminal negligence and the like. The categories "vocational" and "peripheral" as they are used here refer to varieties of crime in which economic gain is an important component.

The explanations of crime submitted by Shaw, McKay, Sutherland, *et al* and refined by Cohen, Cloward and Ohlin, and others, appear to be most appropriate to the interpretation of the behavior of vocational criminals. The explanations need not be discussed here except to note in a general way that in the creation of a full-time vocational criminal, four important factors seem to be involved: (1) a pre-criminal personality structure based on hostility; (2) a strong drive for economic gain and the absence of legitimate channels to economic success; (3) the continuing presence of persons able to instruct the neophyte in the kinds of criminal activity which offer immediate personal rewards, and (4) in-group support which enables the criminal to redefine his values and to attribute legitimacy to behavior considered illegitimate by "official" society.

Once crime has become the person's way of making a living, he continues with a kind of fanatic persistence even though his particular criminal trade brings him into constant and losing conflicts with the agencies of law enforcement. But economic gain is not the only motive for selecting crime as a vocation (or for selecting any other vocation). Many occupational criminals have undergone a kind of Nietzschean "transvaluation of values" in which open flouting of law becomes a mark of cleverness in the criminal in-group and brings a kind of superior status to the successful thief which sometimes is more important to him than the money or merchandise he has stolen. He may fritter away money, but the fact that he has "pulled off" an imaginative coup (in, say, Willie Sutton's style) has enhanced his reputation. By committing successful thefts he becomes, at last, someone to reckon with rather than someone who can be ignored or rejected. "Bravado" acts of theft bring status in the world of the vocational thief, a world in which the conventional values of society stand on their heads.

Vocational thieves appear to be, however, a minority of all thieves. Most people who steal maintain conventional attitudes toward theft as such and toward the merchandise or money stolen. Their crimes are peripheral to rather than central to their lives. Embezzlers, white collar criminals, till-tappers, skippers, and pilferers probably outnumber all other categories of the criminal population, but their goal is to enhance middle-class status, not reject it, to be "pro-social" as Cressey puts it, not "anti-social." When theft does not accomplish this result, and apprehension or arrest threatens the goal, theft will be abandoned as a means to the goal. The difference in reformability between the peripheral, "respectable" thieves, and the vocational thieves supports this hypothesis. Once arrested, pilferers stop pilfering, but vocational thieves persist in spite of repeated arrests and severe penalties.

The peripheral criminal has a vocation which is legitimate. His career may be in merchandising, clerical work, teaching, machine operating, nursing, truck driving, police work, medicine. His major source of livelihood is from his respectable career and he identifies with the dominant values of society. In the course of his life, however, he may perceive opportunities to enhance his income or augment his possessions through misrepresentation, larceny, fraud, embezzlement, receiving stolen property, shoplifting, bribe giving or taking, etc. His perception of opportunities may be sharpened by a personal financial crisis or they may be constantly present. But his criminal acts are not as important to him as his central vocational and status-achieving occupation. Because acts of theft or fraud are incidental to his total career, he rationalizes these acts to conform to his (usually middle-class) system of values. Conventionally oriented people who commit larceny cannot even reveal to their friends or family that their money or possessions have been acquired by stealing. They try to maintain images of themselves as superior bargain hunters, better shoppers, trusted and highly paid employees. They dissemble even to themselves. "I'll put the money back when I can afford it." "It isn't really stealing, its just borrowing." "The company is rich; they'll never miss the little I take." "I've helped to make this business what it is. I deserve some of the gravy."

When arrest (private or public) forces these peripheral thieves to "face up" to the fictions they have espoused, they are temporarily defenseless and panic stricken.

Whereas a specific criminal act or series of acts can be partially rationalized by the person with an established and conventional self-image, a full time vocation of criminal behavior cannot be. The thief who is oriented toward middle-class values feels that his associates would scorn him if his law violations are publicly exposed. His central occupational career and main source of livelihood will be jeopardized. His family, for whom he believes he should have been a model of good conduct, may despise or reject him. Hence, when apprehended in a criminal act he (or she) will go to any length to keep the arrest private. He will offer restitution, accept a downgrading of status, or agree to be discharged from his employment without protest. Since his crimes occur in settings in which private police detect them, these solutions can be achieved "outside the law." And the respectably oriented law violator seldom appears in public records.

When forced to reveal their law violations to their families, however some of these clandestine thieves find more understanding and more personal support for themselves (although not for their thefts) within their families and among their friends than they had expected. They are not totally rejected although they may be harshly treated. Some of them find, in time, that the experience even of unofficial arrest has left them feeling more secure and more protected than before, and therefore, perhaps, psychologically, less impelled to steal again. For young shoplifters, especially, this point should not be overlooked.

THE SPECIAL PROBLEM OF THE YOUNG OFFENDER

Shoplifting, as the data show, is disproportionately a crime of young people. The data also seem to indicate that noncommercial shoplifting continues until the experience of arrest forces the shoplifter either to abandon the practice or to reconsider the attitudes he will have toward the maintenance of a respectable social status. This naturally leads us to wonder whether private police practices do not have within them a general preventive potential insofar as the younger offender is concerned. If so, could it be realized in a practical way?

Apprehension for shoplifting is a very frequent first brush with the law for young people. The experience often has a traumatic impact that may have real significance in their lives. If the young shoplifter can believe that he has a great deal to lose by continuing to steal, he stops stealing just as the older shoplifter does. His belief, however, must be grounded in reality, and many young people are necessarily confused as to where their status lies. If the young pilferer has a family which, in effect, gathers around him and says, "You didn't *have* to steal things; we like you just as you are," and if by implication, the family adds "but never do this again or you'll be in real trouble, you'll have a police record and you'll never get a job or be able to finish high school or do any of the things we had hoped you'd be able to do," these reactions represent for the younger as well as for the adult pilferer a kind of unexpected support which will help to keep him from repeating his offense. Whether or not family-type punishments short of total rejection add to or detract from the preventive value of the arrest experience is at present a matter of pure conjecture. The young person with firm middle-class status aspirations is, we can surmise, little different in this respect from his older counterpart and behaves in a similar way.

Not every young person, however, has a *real* status which is threatened by arrest. Many children and adolescents reared in the "underprivileged" areas of cities have, in their own eyes, *no* status at all; and they have strong reasons to reject the conventional channels to success. In their own world two value structures compete for their allegiance. They have seen examples of adults in their own neighborhoods who have achieved considerable "success" in the criminal rackets. Such examples are inescapable in slum areas where the well-dressed local man in a fine, new car is almost sure to be someone who is engaged in a criminal career, and the best dressed and most attractive young women are likely to be call girls. They have also seen the economic and personal difficulties which beset the lives of relatives and neighbors who are honest, hard working and law abiding citizens.

Career choices are not, of course, made on a calculated rational basis, but a realistic appraisal of the prospects for success and upward mobility can hardly lead the urban slum boy or girl to a firm conviction that crime does not pay when, in fact, it sometimes pays rather well. Crime as an occupation, moreover, does not require a college degree or even a high school diploma.

Nevertheless young people also know something of the risks and deprivations involved in extra-legal success and they have observed successful aspirants to respectability (teachers, social workers, civil servants, police, nurses, lawyers, doctors, etc.). The career decision which has to be made by the slum-reared young man or woman is thus of greater moment than that of his middle-class contemporary who can, still, be thrown into a minor panic when he must chose between law and dentistry. Bloch and Niederhoffer say:

The lower-class boy . . . absorbs dominant middle-class values which set goals for him, but sees on every hand that he is unable to pursue these ends. To many a lower-class boy socially approved objectives for desired manhood are so far-fetched, so unattainable, that they constitute a sort of chimera, a never-never land about which he can dream but actually not hope to achieve. The patterns of living of his father and other adult male figures in his environment appear to offer testimony as to the futility of achieving goals which the popular cult of American success so stridently affirms in the classroom, the movies, TV, and other popular channels of mass enlightenment. What models are offered in the lives of parents and others in his environment, who are closely bound to a limited and constricted routine of seemingly unrewarded toil, appear uninspired and, for many youths, hardly worth the effort. Recognizing the limitations on his strivings, the values of the working-class youth may be an actual negation of the very things which the calculated prudence of the middle class hopes to foster among its own young.[5]

In spite of the seeming attractiveness of a criminal career, most young people (slum-reared or otherwise) chose the lesser risk by conforming to conventional demands; although this conformity for many slum-reared children leads only to one dreary and difficult job after another rather than into a spiral of increasing responsibilities, increasing status, and increasing rewards. Sometimes they are rejected by criminal in-groups as lacking the initiative, trustworthiness, and cunning needed for a criminal career.

The slum-reared boy or girl in his initial encounters with law enforcement agencies is apt to be balanced on a tightrope:

These early acts of deviance are in effect tentative steps toward the adoption of norms in competition with the official rules. At this stage the deviant needs all the encouragement and reassurance he can muster to defend his position. He finds these by searching out others who have faced similar experiences and who will support one another in common attitudes of alienation from the official system. The deviant who is unable to mobilize such social support will have great difficulty in establishing firm grounds for his defiance of the official system, for he requires not only justifying beliefs but also social validation of the appropriateness of his deviant acts.

The initial contest between the individual and the authorities over the legitimacy of certain social norms and the appropriate-

5. Bloch, Herbert and Arthur Niederhoffer. *The Gang: A Study in Adolescent Behavior.* (New York, 1958), p. 109.

ness of certain acts of deviance sets in motion a process of definition that marks the offender as different from law-abiding folk. His acts and his person are defined as "evil," and he is caught up in a vicious cycle of norm-violation, repression, resentment, and new and more serious acts of violation. The process of alienation is accelerated, and the chasm between the offender and those who would control and reform him grows wider and deeper. In such circumstances he becomes increasingly dependent on the support of others in his position. The gang of peers forms a new social world in which the legitimacy of his delinquent conduct is strongly reinforced.[6]

Although motivated initially by the same acquisitive desires as his middle-class peers, the slum-reared adolescent may, however, respond to arrest for shoplifting not by tearful imploring but by a show of hardness and cynicism which invites further retribution. The store detective has been hired to protect merchandise. It seems perfectly obvious to him that the "young toughs" of both sexes need to be taught a lesson and that only public officials are equipped to teach this lesson. A store protection official thus tends to push the prosecution in such cases as hard as it can be pushed. Commitment to a reform institution or jail is frequently the outcome.

Having been able to enjoy the benefits of a juvenile penal institution, however, the "young tough" indeed learns a number of lessons. He (or she) learns to stay away from "kid stuff" like pilfering and "get wise" to the real rackets. He learns where merchandise can be sold; and where stolen merchandise can be pawned. He learns the kinds of things to take and, he learns to hate and fear all legal authority. In short, he learns to be a "booster" or to follow some other criminal trade.

6. Cloward and Ohlin, *Op. cit.*, pp. 126–127.

The firm dramatization of the "evil" which separates the child out of his group for specialized treatment plays a greater role in making the criminal than perhaps any other experience. It cannot be too often emphasized that for the child the whole situation has become different. He now lives in a different world. He has been tagged. A new and hitherto nonexistent environment has been precipitated out for him.

The process of making the criminal, therefore, is a process of tagging, defining, indentifying, segregating, describing, emphasizing, making conscious and self-conscious; it becomes a way of stimulating, suggesting emphasizing, and evolving the very traits that are complained of. If the theory of relation of response to stimulus has any meaning, the entire process of dealing with the young delinquent is mischievous in so far as it identifies him to himself or to the environment as a delinquent person.[7]

When the process of identifying the child to himself and to his environment as a delinquent simultaneously equips him with the attitudes and skills of an extra-legal trade that has immediate rewards and the possibility of increasing "success," he is well set on a career that is difficult or impossible to reverse.

But is this process inevitable? Because of the special position of private police, they encounter thousands of young people every year. Many of these youngsters are on the verge of criminal careers. Is it impossible for stores and other businesses who support private police, also, in their own self interest, to support private programs of individual reform in which both public and private police, sociologists, guidance counsellors and others cooperate? These programs need not be aimed at those thieves whose *real* status has been so threatened by unofficial arrest that

7. Tannenbaum, Frank. *Crime and the Community.* (New York, 1938), pp. 19–20.

they will cease stealing without further help. They should be directed rather toward the creation of legitimate status for the young people who lack it—the "young toughs" not yet committed to crime as a vocation, but not yet secure in any other way of life.

Admittedly the problem is difficult, but presently available avenues of reform for this group are usually dead-end streets. Institutions for youthful offenders, for example, report rates of recidivism of 50 per cent or more (and these rates do not include the people who continue to steal but are not caught).

While it is premature even to suggest the outline of a program that might be economically rewarding as well as humanitarian, businesses with inventory shrinkages of $100,000 a year or more could well afford inquisitive attitudes and pooling of financial resources for experimental purposes. It seems probable that they would within a few years begin to get substantial returns on their initial investments.

SOURCES OF DATA

STORE DATA

In the eight years, 1943 through 1950, Lakeside Co. store detectives arrested approximately 4,600 men, women, and children for shoplifting. These people were questioned at length by trained and experienced interrogators, and information relevant to the interests of the store protection staff was recorded. The data of this study consist in part, of this information as recorded for every fourth person arrested selected chronologically by arrest. The data cards were prepared under my direction by the store protection staff for use in this study. They were copies of the original records save for the deletion of the names of arrested people and identifying addresses.

Relatively little interview material could be gathered, and the kind of information that might have been gained from interviews with arrested shoplifters would have been of considerable value. In point of fact, it was impossible to obtain. Shoplifters who were apprehended in the store were either to be prosecuted in the court and thus believed that any statement they made would be used in legal process or they were to be released after interrogation by the store detectives. In the latter instance they had been through such an intense emotional experience that they were unable or unwilling to communicate. In any event, the day of arrest is not a day on which information useful to a research worker can be elicited from an arrested person when the research worker has no legal right to ask the necessary questions.

Recorded information which was available included for each person (and records were almost always complete) the following:

(1) *Sex*.

(2) *Address*: recorded as, e.g., 57–6 Kimbark instead of 5716 Kimbark. This type of recording permitted spot mapping by census tract or census area, but at the same time an address did not betray the exact location of the arrested person's residence. This recording means was both entirely adequate for research purposes, and at the same time in line with the store's policy of protecting the anonymity of arrested persons.

(3) *Time*: hour of arrest.

(4) *Alias*: recorded as plus or minus indicating whether or not an alias was used by the shoplifter (and, of course, discovered by store officials).

(5) *Employment*: recorded as given by the arrested person.

(6) *Marital status*: single, married, widowed, divorced.

(7) *Spouse's occupation*: employment, if any, of the spouse. Given in the same manner as "employment" above.

(8) *Accomplices*: given in terms of the number, sex, and age of each.

(9) *Disposition*: disposition of the case; i.e., release by the store or placing of formal charge for arrest by the police department. If formal charge was placed, the outcome of court procedures.

(10) *Previous record*: had the person been arrested previously by any of the other nine "State Street" department

stores that kept cooperative records, or did the person have a known police record? Police records were known only for persons who admitted them or who were formally charged with larceny.

(11) *Tip:* was the person arrested as a result of a "tip off" to the protection department from a sales person, floor manager, etc.?

(12) *Age:* as given by the shoplifter.

(13) *Weight:* as given by the shoplifter.

(14) *Height:* as given by the shoplifter.

(15) *Nationality:* recorded in terms of national ancestry or racial, and sometimes religious background, e.g., German-American, Irish-Swedish, Negro, Jewish, etc.

(16) *Merchandise recovered:* Itemized listing of the stolen merchandise recovered from the shoplifter, e.g., pin, belt, gloves, etc.

(17) *Value of merchandise stolen:* total value only of all merchandise listed above; no values were given for individual items. However values were listed according to the price tag value of the merchandise, not, as in Court records where store merchandise valued at $15.00 or more had to be considered grand larceny and require a more time-consuming court procedure than charges of petty larceny.

(18) *Merchandise from other stores:* if the person had merchandise stolen from other stores in his possession, the name of the store, itemization of the merchandise and the total value of the merchandise.

COMPLETENESS AND ACCURACY OF INFORMATION

All of the information itemized above was recorded for most of the persons arrested. The portion of the information which constituted the potential base for legal action against the shoplifter was, of course, recorded fully, and, no doubt, accurately. This included the date, time, nature of stolen merchandise, value of stolen merchandise, sex, and age (as between juvenile and adult—age 18 being the dividing year). The information on age (other than above or below 18), address, height and weight, employment, nationality, marital status, and whether or not the person attempted to use an alias was, of course, subject to whatever inaccuracy the shoplifter, for one reason or another, introduced, but in as much as the shoplifter was subject to intensive interrogation and all identification papers carried by the arrested person were thoroughly examined, it is unlikely that many inaccuracies could have occurred in this material.

Since the material on height and weight was not used in this study, inaccuracy is of no consequence. "Nationality" was used only as Negro and white. Age was often given in round numbers (50, 55, 60). Marital status was, especially for women, examined by store detectives with some care. Interrogators could ascertain prior records for women only if names in prior marriages were known.

The three items of information in which inaccuracies could appear that were of consequence in this study were: address, employment, prior criminal record.

Addresses. A small proportion of addresses given by arrested persons was certainly false. How large was this proportion, it is impossible to estimate. It is unlikely that it was as much as five per cent, for, as noted before, identification papers were examined if the shoplifter carried them. If not, the probability was that the shoplifter would have been formally charged, and thus subject to police inquiry after which accurate information would have been recorded in store archives. Local addresses were especially significant

in this study since these data were collected in Chicago
where, over the years, the University of Chicago (and the
Chicago Community Inventory) had compiled highly useful information about all phases of the social and economic
composition of local neighborhoods.

Employment. The recording of occupations of shoplifters was sometimes incomplete and because questions on
this subject were not of vital concern to the store protection department, they were not handled with the care
normally demanded by a social analyst. Answers were
sometimes recorded either in terms of the place of employment or in terms of the kind of work. Considerable numbers of men stated that they were unemployed. Some of
them probably feared that employers would be informed
of the arrest and thus might have had adequate motivation to withhold employment information.

COURT DATA

The second collection of data used in this study, I took
from the books of the Chicago Municipal Court (Branch
40; also called Women's Court) for the years 1948, 1949,
and 1950. To this court come for initial hearing all *women*
charged with misdemeanors in Chicago. (Women charged
with felonies go to other courts.) Women misdemeanants
who waive jury trial are all tried in this court. Male misdemeanants are tried in many branch courts dispersed
throughout the city. Hence virtually all cases of arrest for
shoplifting by women are tried in this court, and for those
few (about half a dozen in the three years under consideration) who demanded jury trial, the initial procedures

are recorded as part of the Women's Court records.* Perhaps a few women were charged with shoplifting as a felony (grand larceny) and not as a misdemeanor. Their records would then not appear as part of the records of this court. Heads of protection bureaus at four leading department stores were questioned on this point and could not recall having so charged any women. Practically, it was impossible to check this point further, for shoplifting does not appear in court books as a separate offense but as one among any number of other crimes that come under the heading of larceny.

During the years 1948–1950 petty larceny included the theft of money or merchandise valued at less than $15.00. (In 1951 the law was revised to include theft of up to $50.00 as petty larceny.) For the purpose of charging shoplifters, the value of merchandise was arbitrarily set at $14.95 by stores when the stolen merchandise was worth this much or more. The reason for the stores' dealing with shoplifting as petty rather than grand larceny is, of course, the decreased energy and time of the store detectives and of legal staffs consumed in preparing the case, in arraignments, and in testifying in the court. This is general practice in other cities as well as in Chicago.

To obtain the data which make up the "Court sample" it was necessary to start with the "court sheets." These are the large sheets of paper used by the Clerk of the

* A note of thanks is in order for the, then, custodian of the records of that court. The records are kept in a vault far in the depths of the court building. The dust necessitated the use of goggles, dust mask, etc., as the records were disturbed, each unfolded and examined. The attendant kindly loaned me the use of his desk, chair, and spittoon. The thanks is especially for the desk and chair which the custodian refrained from using during the several months in which the work was done.

Court. They contain the name, case number, charge, and disposition of the case or other action taken by the court. This information is recorded consecutively for each person appearing before the court regardless of offense. From these court sheets I took the case numbers of all persons charged with petty larceny. Since the handwriting of court clerks varied in legibility, and since petty larceny cases were sometimes recorded as "petty larceny," sometimes as shoplifting, and sometimes as 38–387 (the number of the statute violated) and since they were interspersed with all other misdemeanors, no doubt a certain proportion of charges against shoplifters were overlooked. There is no reason, however, to think that significant selective factors entered into this overlooking.

The "Court sample" is thus composed of almost all women over the age of 18 who were charged with shoplifting by stores within the city of Chicago in the three years 1948, 1949, and 1950. Each charge of petty larceny in the Women's Court was examined individually, and 873 of the total of 1319 cases of women charged with petty larceny were shoplifters. Two hundred and twenty were not. Thus of the known cases of petty larceny of women, 80 per cent were charges of shoplifting. The remaining 226 cases could not, for various reasons, be classified with certainty. For a few there was no arrest slip in the file and others (90 of them) although they had been tried by the court had no record in the files at all. Merchandise had been stolen from a store by 82 women, but it appeared probable that these were store employees. In 27 records goods had been stolen from an individual.

Statistics published by the police department show that in 1948, and this is the only year in which both "court data" and police records were both obtainable, 712 women were charged with larceny in Chicago. In this study 508 cases were examined for that year. Thus the data here fail to account for 204 cases of women charged with larceny. Some of these were grand larceny cases rather than shoplifting and hence not under the jurisdiction of the Women's Court. Others could have been overlooked in the court "books," or have been misfiled.

The information in the file for each woman consisted of, first, the "arrest slip," a form filled in by the arresting police officer. On it the name, address, alias (if ascertained), race, age, occupation, height, weight, sex, marital status (in terms only of married or single), complexion, date and time of police arrest. It also contained the charge, place of arrest, the names of the arresting officers, and the name of the complainant or complainants.

Second, the file contained the charge "did with illegal intent take, lead, walk or carry away [specified items of merchandise] the property of [name of owner or corporation] located at [address] of the value of [usually $14.95; or less if the actual was less]." This complaint was signed by the store detective or, in some cases, by the store manager.

Third, the file had in it the report of the probation investigator, if probation had been applied for, and of the psychiatrist, if psychiatric examination had been ordered by the court.

The fourth item in the file was the formal record of the legal procedures in the case; the amount of bond, the date of trial, any continuances asked for and refused or granted, the sentence, the record of any motions to vacate the sentence and the action take on the motion, and the name of the judge. The termination of the sentence was likewise noted as well as the payment of any fines that were assessed.

From these available data, the following items of information were recorded: name, address, age, nationality, occupation, marital status, weight, height, date, time, name of store in which arrest was made, items of merchandise stolen, value of stolen merchandise, whether a psychiatric report was ordered, and if ordered, the report was reproduced, the sentence, motions to vacate any action on the motion, and the name of the judge.

POLICE RECORDS

In addition to the Store and Court records, it was possible through the cooperation of the Police Department to record the prior police records of a number of shoplifters. To make up this sample, 78 women were chosen from the court cases discussed above, and 34 men were selected from the records of the Court Branch 38 (the downtown branch of the Chicago Municipal Court). The use made of these records is discussed in context.

METHOD OF PRESENTATION OF DATA

The method of presentation of the statistical data of this study is governed by two factors; first, the nature of the available data, and second, the relevance of the data to the central purpose of the study.

Nature of the data. The data used for this study were not, as has been pointed out, secured directly from the subjects but were taken from records made for purposes other than this study. If interviews and questionnaires could have been used, more information would also have been secured. Because this was impossible, data on certain interesting questions do not exist. On other questions, sometimes unfortunately those of less sociologcial or psychological interest, data were abundant.

Relevance. The central purpose of this study is not department store protection (nor vocational opportunities for shoplifters), but the contribution of the material to theories of criminal behavior. Some of the data, however, have been found useful for store detectives. (*See* Edwards, Loren, *Shoplifting and Shrinkage Protection for Stores.*) Edwards incorporated data from the study into a didactic volume for store protection staff members. The sociologically relevant information, is however, of four kinds: 1) how shoplifters function as thieves; 2) how they function as persons aside from their thefts; 3) how some of them are selected for official charge; and 4) the effect of arrest in so far as subsequent crime is concerned. For none of these four points is the available evidence all that might be wished, but what does exist is objective, and on certain questions sufficient for the construction of hypotheses.